# Agrarian Reform in Chile

# Agrarian Reform in Chile

An Economic Study

Jeannine Swift *1935—*
State University of New York—
Geneseo

**Heath Lexington Books**
D. C. Heath and Company
Lexington, Massachusetts

# Table of Contents

# List of Tables

# Preface

The implementation of any decision by a democratic government to make a radical change in the institutional structure of its economy must necessarily be constrained by several important factors. These factors in one way or another are related to the fact that a democratic government must retain the support of the majority of the population in order to effectively pursue any policy. Furthermore, any radical change in the institutional structure of an economy will almost certainly benefit some at the expense of others. A decision to make such a change must consider the number and political power of those who will benefit as against the number and political power of those at whose expense the benefits will be obtained. Regardless of the ultimate "justice" of a certain policy, it simply cannot be implemented by a democratic government without political support. The implementation of policy is further complicated by the fact that political support or the lack thereof will be dominated by the short-run effects of a policy with little regard for possible differences between short-run and long-run effects.

The decision by the government of Chile to initiate and execute an agrarian reform is a decision to effect a radical change in the pattern of land ownership. As such, its implementation is constrained by the factors mentioned above. Therefore, any evaluation of the reform must identify the particular constraints under which the government of Chile must operate and take these factors into account when judging whether or not the program is successful.

It is the intention of this preface to offer the author's personal judgement of the program for agrarian reform adopted by Chile in 1964. This judgement is made with every effort to take into account the constraints within which those responsible for executing the program have had to operate.

It will be helpful to begin by explaining the specific constraints which must be kept in mind in this evaluation. The first of these is that faced by any economy: resources are limited and only a certain percent of these resources can be devoted to any particular goal. In principle, an agrarian reform, that is to say a reorganization of land ownership patterns, could be nearly costless in its implementation. The law could simply transfer ownership from those who currently own the land to the farm laborers. This could be done without compensation to the present land owners, or with compensation to be paid by the new recipients of land. Changes in infrastructure use could be left up to the new landowners to work out for themselves. In Chile these changes would mean reorganizing the irrigation facilities and determining the use of machinery, buildings, and equipment. Since such a plan would probably result in chaos, the decision must be made about how much organizational staff is needed and how much government help will be given to reorganize the infrastructure and capital equipment. Once this decision is made, the number of farms which may be transferred annually is limited by the amount of the government budget allocated for this purpose.

The second constraint, which is not necessarily true of all economies, is imposed by the fact that the Chilean economy cannot sustain a decrease in the marketed agricultural production. With only about one-third of the labor force in the agricultural sector, this sector must supply the remainder of the labor force with food. The food supply in Chile is already problematic as will be seen in the body of this study. The need for increased agricultural production was given as one of the major reasons for the need for an agrarian reform. It is doubtful, therefore, that sufficient support for the reform can be sustained unless such an increase is forthcoming. In what way does the need to insure an increase in marketed agricultural production constrain the agrarian reform program? Several factors are involved. The recipients of land, long accustomed to receiving orders and making no management decisions, cannot be expected to become efficient farm managers in a short period of time. Thus, some method of training prior to transfer of ownership must be provided if output is not to decline. A second factor is that the recipients of land, accustomed in the past to low levels of consumption, may be expected to increase their own food consumption. Unless agricultural output is increased to accommodate the increased food consumption on the farm, less, instead of more, will be available to the two-thirds of the labor force who live in the urban sector. The program for agrarian reform must be organized in such a way as to provide incentives to the land recipients to produce more for the market. The third factor is that the new recipients of land will not have the capital necessary for production. They will not normally be "good" credit risks. Some mechanism for handling credit facilitation must be built in to the reform program. Thus the need to maintain and even to increase agricultural production places limitations on the *kind* of reform possible and the speed with which it may be implemented. This need also requires that owners whose land is not at the moment expropriated be given incentives to continue production.

The final, and perhaps the most important constraint to be treated here is that imposed by the human fact that people must work with people. If the land ownership is simply transferred to the farm workers, they must, as a group, agree on the reorganization of irrigation facilities or work out ways to cooperate in the use of existing facilities. If these decisions are made at a higher level, someone must explain the decisions and persuade the workers to accept them. If there is to be a management training program, someone must, in effect, be a teacher. Furthermore the recipients of land must be persuaded to wait until the training program is over before receiving their land. In Chile, personnel are needed who can persuade some workers to move. One of the problems in Chilean agriculture is that some farms are overcrowded, others have insufficient workers. The need to transfer families and the need to persuade persons on understaffed farms to accept new workers requires personal communication. The success of these efforts is constrained by the number of people who are able to teach, to influence, and to communicate ideas to other people.

In view of these three constraints, the author here presents a personal judgement of the agrarian reform in Chile. A radical restructuring of land ownership was defined by law to mean that 100,000 families would become land owners. The major part of this goal was to be accomplished by 1970. (The reader should be reminded that the total population of Chile is less than nine million and that only one-third are in agriculture. The number, 100,000, refers to families, not to individuals. It does involve, therefore, a fairly sizeable proportion of the total rural population.) It is doubtful that more than 20,000 families will be involved before the election in September 1970. Simply in terms of this goal, the radical change is far from having been accomplished. The following questions are raised by this failure to reach the stated goal. Was the goal unrealistic? Could more have been achieved and, if so, how? Is there anything other countries can learn from the Chilean experience? Finally, what is the future for Chile, will the goal ever be reached?

Given the constraints discussed above, the goal was probably unrealistic. Individual farms had to be visited and evaluated. Before a training for management program could be started, a staff had to be trained to implement such a program. Short of a mood of urgency, which cannot be expected of a peacetime democratic country, this mobilization effort simply could not have been of sufficient scale and speed to organize 100,000 families in the period from 1964 to 1970. The constraint was not primarily the budget size, but rather one of logistics.

But there are ways in which more could have been accomplished. Too much attention in the early stage of the reform was given to housing. Though, by American standards, houses of farm workers were primitive, small, dark, and in need of repair, the workers were not wholly unsatisfied with them. The building of houses consumed time and resources. The officials responsible felt that such housing should be provided in order to maintain the support of the workers. (It may seem strange that such support was needed. As will become clear later the need for a training program prior to transfer of ownership required that workers wait and be "tested" for three years before receiving a guarantee that the land would be theirs.) I do not think the housing program was necessary, or even helpful, in acquiring worker support. In some cases, it did just the opposite. The houses were built closer together than that to which the workers were accustomed and they preferred their former privacy. Concern about housing could have waited for a much later stage. Time and resources could have been saved here.

A second element is that too much time was given to analyzing the possibilities of the farm before it was expropriated. This detailed projection of what the farm could produce either should not have been made or it should have been used. The officials should have recognized early that these plans could not be enforced on the workers after the farm was expropriated or else recognized that more firmness was needed and enforced their use. Time and resources were used up in making these plans and the morale of those who made them suffered when they were not used.

Thirdly, insufficient attention was given to the training of staff in how to work with people. A large number of staff workers are engaged in educating former workers in the methods of farm management. This type of education requires an ability to handle human relations and to influence without dominating, talents few people have naturally. Attention to this problem should have been incorporated in the staff training. It is the author's contention that the basic problem of human communication is the most serious obstacle to the success of the Chilean reform and will be for any other country that attempts such a reform. It is not something peculiar to Chile, it is part of the larger problem of man's inability to deal effectively with other men.

The future of agrarian reform in Chile will probably be determined in the September 1970 elections. Because of the factors discussed above, the reform has fallen far short of reaching its stated goal. In its present form, therefore, it is not likely to have sufficient political support. Nevertheless, not an insignificant number of people have been affected. Although the change has not been thorough, there has been a change. Furthermore, it has been demonstrated that radical change *is* possible via democratic institutions. Other countries *could* learn from the Chilean experience if they wish to implement a similar program.

Up to this point all judgements have been made with regard to the achievement of the goals of agrarian reform as stated by Chile. This study was conducted in the same spirit. There has been no attempt to question whether or not agrarian reform is a good thing in itself. The answer to such a question involves personal opinions and value judgements, which research tries to avoid. For the benefit of the reader who wishes to know, however, I will in this preface state my opinion on this question.

There are two parts to the question. One part concerns social justice. The other part concerns a choice to be made among various alternatives for accomplishing a given economic objective. This writer thinks that agrarian reform is a good policy with relation to both parts. In Chile, as well as in many other countries, the farm worker is very close to serfdom. The house he lives in belongs to the landowner who assumes the right to control visitors from outside his farm. Produce from the small garden plot he is given as part payment for his labor may not be marketed unless the landowner so decides. Wages are so low that there is no hope of ever saving enough to escape or buy land of his own. In any case, land is rarely for sale. We regard this situation as unjust. It is no help to argue that some landowners are "kind"—give Christmas presents, extend credit, and allow the workers to watch TV in the landowners own house. This is not conducive to human dignity. From the point of view of breaking the stranglehold on the rural laboring class, agrarian reform is a desirable policy. On the other hand, social justice is hardly served by indirectly making the urban working class pay for the reform in agriculture through inflation or cutbacks in spending on public services. A redistribution of income or wealth should be from those who have to those who have not, and not from the urban have nots to the rural have nots. Such a redistribution implies either that full compensation not be given for expropriated land or that compensation be postponed until the recipients can pay for the land themselves. As will be seen in this study, Chile did manage a law which only partially compensated landowners, but because of what the author regards as an insufficient firmness in the treatment of prospective land recipients, the urban sector has indirectly been penalized for the benefit of these recipients.

As an aggregate economic policy, agrarian reform has been posed as a method to improve resource use. If land is more of a status symbol than a profit-making venture, then it will not necessarily be used efficiently. There is some presumption that if the present working class were given the land they could not afford to take status as an alternative to profits. As will be seen in Chapter 2 of this study, the evidence regarding the efficiency of land use by owners of large tracts of land as opposed to land use by owners of family-sized farms is not clear. In the face of evidence that is controversial, one must still make judgements about what to do. Personal experience in Chile leads us to make the judgement that it is indeed true that a sizeable amount of good land is not used or is very inefficiently used. The transfer of ownership of this land at the least would make things no worse. There is good reason to believe that at least some of this land would be used more efficiently if ownership were transferred. An alternative to an agrarian reform to accomplish the objective to better land use is a well-conceived land tax. Such a tax would be based on productive possibilities rather than on actual production. This would presumably force land owners to produce or sell. In terms of sheer economic efficiency, a tax policy is probably more desirable than agrarian reform. The economist must bow to the political scientist for answers to the question of which is more politically possible. But in terms of overall social development, agrarian reform appears to be the more desirable policy.

The criticisms made in this preface and in the body of the study are therefore made in a constructive spirit and are not intended to imply that the author thinks the program should be halted. It is regrettable that the present government had such a short time to learn from its own mistakes and was harassed by a severe draught in 1968 and 1969. Has enough been accomplished in the last six years to effect a permanent shift in structure of land ownership and the social position of the rural laboring class? Only the future can supply the answer to this question.

One final question to which this preface should address itself is the present usefulness of the results in Chapters 5 and 6. The research for this study was completed in 1968. The production on *asentamientos* is that for the agricultural year 1966–1967. Since that time CORA has made efforts to deal with some of the problems experienced in its first few years of operation. Of what value, then, is the publication of these earlier results? The results on production (Chapter 5) are primarily of historical interest. A study, using more current production data, is needed in order to judge whether or not production has begun to change significantly since 1967. Because the data collection of CORA has been more systematic since 1967, such a study would be easier than the one completed here. Comparisons, however, would be complicated by the fact that Chile experienced severe draughts in 1968 and 1969. In the original plan for the revision of this study we had hoped to obtain more recent production data. But the draught, together with political complications made such a revision implausible at the present time. Projections concerning the impact of *asentamiento* production on the aggregate economy in both Chapters 5 and 6 were based on a projection made in 1968 of the number of families to be in *asentamientos* by 1970. The number of families actually in *asentamientos* on December 31, 1969 was only about one-half the number we had projected. It is doubtful, therefore, that whatever happens to production on *asentamientos* can significantly affect total agricultural output at the present time. It is also improbable that the redistribution impact of the reform can yet be felt in the industrial sector. The number of families is still too small relative to the total rural population. However, the basic concepts discussed in Chapters 5 and 6 are still valid. If expropriations are continued after 1971, the impact originally projected for 1971 may still be felt at a later date.

# Acknowledgments

This book, with minor revisions, was first written as a dissertation completed in the department of economics at the Massachusetts Institute of Technology. I wish to express my gratitude to Professor Rosenstein-Rodan for his help and encouragement in the initial stages of formulating this study. Professors Matthew Edel, Richard Eckaus, and Everett Hagan provided valuable encouragement and criticism as the work progressed.

It is always difficult for an American student to do field research in another culture. Without the cooperation of Eduardo Garcia of ODEPLAN and Ramon Downey of CORA, this work would never have been possible. Arthur Jolly of ICIRA, whose friendship and assistance were a continual support, deserves special thanks. The warmth, kindness, and generosity of the dozens of Chilean people with whom I talked and among whom I lived not only provided insight and information for the study completed here, but also helped make the research an enjoyable, human experience.

Financial support was gratefully received from the Ford Foundation Dissertation Fellowship program for my year in Chile and from a teaching assistantship at MIT during the year completing the dissertation. The conclusions and opinions of this study, however, are those of the author alone and are not necessarily shared by those who provided financial support nor by those who cooperated in any way with this research.

Americans are by now familiar with the large concentrations of urban workers on the outskirts of large Latin American cities. In Chile these are known as "poblaciónes." To the five Sisters of Loretto, living in the midst of Población José María Caro, I offer my most sincere thanks for providing me with a home in Chile.

To Judith Ford, my roommate in Cambridge, I am deeply grateful. In the midst of writing her own dissertation, she provided encouragement and support for the original study, and has also helped in the editing and preparation of the draft for publication.

# 1 Introduction

"Economists are more and more agreed that an agrarian reform is actually a fundamental institutional precondition in order to continue and to accelerate the process of development in Latin America."[1]

These words of the vice president of the Institute for Agricultural Development in Chile state an attitude which indeed has become more widespread in the last several years. And yet very little careful study has been made to substantiate the relationship between the institutional structure that now exists and the process of development. What has become evident in the last few years is that support of industrial development by a developing country does not necessarily imply that agricultural development will keep pace. In a strictly competitive model in which agricultural supply is price elastic, the amount supplied would be increased when an improvement in the price of products resulted from increased demand in the urban sector; i.e., agricultural development would keep pace.

But in the real world of underdeveloped or developing countries the perfectly competitive model does not always work. Pushing industrial development has not in fact resulted in an agricultural development which keeps pace. As a consequence, the increased demand for food has created inflationary pressure and balance-of-payments problems, which have in turn put brakes on, or at least distorted the pattern of industrial development. It is imperative, then, to ask the question: Why is it that agricultural supply has not kept pace with demand? Where is the imperfection in the system? There are two opposing views on this question.

One view, put forth in recent years by economists who agree with Chonchol, is that the pattern of ownership of land is the source of the imperfection.[2] This view is based on the assumption that the owners of large landholdings in many underdeveloped countries and in particular in Latin America, hold land more for a status symbol than for profit making. Therefore the large landholder is not necessarily moved by profit incentives as is usually meant in the theory of the firm. This is not to say that he is irrational. It is simply that his farm gives him another sort of "income" than money income, that is, status, a summer home, or a hedge against inflation. Supply, then, of agricultural products from these farmers is relatively inelastic: large increases in price would be required to provide the incentive to put forth the effort necessary for increasing output.

From the small landholder there is even less hope of obtaining a greater supply of foodstuffs. Credit channels are rarely open to him except at high premiums, and he cannot purchase the necessary additional seed, fertilizer, etc. without credit. If, as one would expect, he is already using land rather intensively, he needs to change his technology immediately, using more fertilizer and better seeds to obtain an increase in output. He often does not even have access to information which would encourage this sort of investment.

To avoid problems of climatic influences, estimates of supply response in agriculture have consistently used as a dependent variable the amount of cropland in seed. Most studies have indicated that indeed the area planted in specific crops does respond strongly to price changes.[3] However, what Latin America needs is an increase in a large number of crops and not simply a change in the relative amounts of specific crops. Expansion of area in this sense is rarely open to the small-sized farms in areas of highly unequal land distribution.

The opposing view of the stagnation in Latin American agriculture is that governments have prevented development by their policies. Price controls on agricultural products, it is argued, have kept profits, and therefore output, low. Farm owners are highly rational, in the traditional economist's sense, and will respond strongly and quickly to profit incentive.[4]

These two views contain an implicit assumption about the degree of elasticity that farm owners have with respect to price. There is also in the arguments an implied value of supply price elasticity that is considered *appropriate,* but this value is never mentioned. The first view contends that supply elasticity is low, implying that if farmers truly maximized profits it would be high. The second view holds that price elasticities are high, and that farmers respond strongly and quickly to price changes. Underlying both arguments is some standard for calling an elasticity high or low.

Any statement about the size of supply elasticity raises an empirical question that cannot be settled by argument. With the exception of one study on coffee in Brazil [5] the analyses of supply thus far have been made in areas where the problem of land use and distribution is quite different from that existing in Latin America. The main thrust of these studies has been to test whether or not subsistence farmers respond to price changes. Behrman indicates in his study, for example, that the number of absentee landlords was quite small and that the land distribution pattern was not unduly skewed.[6] Inasmuch as the present study is concerned with agrarian reform in Chile, where the majority of agricultural products do not come from subsistence farmers and where the land distribution is quite skewed, it will deal with a slightly different problem than did previous studies of supply response.

There is one further aspect of this problem which should be considered. Let us suppose that supply has some price elasticity. Then the amount of food supplied in the market would increase food products. But food products are an important part of the budget of the industrial work force. Rising food prices for a given money wage will therefore decrease the real wage. If wage earners are able to insist through strikes on higher money wages in order to maintain their real wage, there are two possible responses by profit makers. Either prices in the industrial sector are increased or profits are allowed to decrease. In fact, if the terms of trade between agricultural and industrial products are to be improved in order to obtain the desired supply increase, and if real wages are to be maintained, then industrial profits must decrease. However, if reinvested profits are the main source of investment, then growth considerations would demand that profits do not decrease. There exist some optimum terms of trade between agriculture and industry which will not only encourage agricultural production, but also allow industry to pay a low money wage without being subject to strikes. In this case, the higher the elasticity of supply of agricultural products, the lower the price needed to get the output desired.

The question of the structure of ownership then becomes: Is it possible that supply would be *more* elastic merely if the structure of ownership were changed? If so, a government could continue to control prices and still get increases in food production. Then we would be concerned with the relative supply responsiveness of present landowners as opposed to that of other possible owners.

Why is there any reason to believe that a change in the structure of land ownership would change the elasticity of supply of food products? In the type of landholding structure in which operational units are rented and the renter pays a portion of the crop to the landlord for the use of the land, the marginal revenue to the renter is equal to his marginal cost at a lower level of operation than if he paid either a fixed land payment or owned the land himself. So if this particular arrangement existed, there would be every reason to expect that an increase in output would result from merely making owners out of the present renters. The land reform in Japan after World War II seems to be a clear case of this type.[7] But the type of arrangement which exists in Chile is that of large landowners who operate the farm either directly or through an administrator with hired labor. Why, then, would there be any reason to anticipate that an increase in supply elasticity would result from making owners out of workers in Chile? The argument has most often been posed in somewhat the following form: Farm ownership pinpoints rather strongly the question, sometimes raised in economics, of why *should an* entrepreneur have such a simple goal as to maximize profits? Why does he not balance the marginal disutility of work with the marginal utility of additional income? In short, inasmuch as a landowner, in order to operate a farm, must put forth a great deal of effort, why does he not balance off the marginal utility of the additional income he would receive with the marginal disutility of the amount of work he must put forth? Since owners of large farms do have fairly large incomes, it might be asked whether or not supply elasticity is not as high as it might be because the marginal utility of additional income is low.[8] Solon Barraclough has stated the problem in the following way:

Powerful, often absentee, landowners with an abundant supply of low-cost dependent tenants and laborers have few incentives to change their methods. To do so would require them to become agricultural entrepreneurs and full-time farm managers instead of traditional landlords. The economic risks and sacrifices required would outweigh the return they foresee from such an effort. Most important, many would have to work very much harder, change their way of life and give up their elite position at the apex of the traditional social pyramid. Also it should be recalled that large estate owners already enjoy relatively large incomes by local standards; in economic terms, the marginal utility of additional income is relatively low.[9]

The implication of this type of argument is that owners of smaller, family-sized farms, given the same opportunities for credit, marketing facilities, etc., would put forth more effort in the operation of a farm. Thus the elasticity of supply would increase if large landholdings were broken up into smaller ownership units, other conditions being equal. But other conditions are not the same for small and large landowners at the present time. There is, therefore, no practical way to test the above hypothesis. If conditions were the same, one could simply test the difference between the supply elasticities of different sized farms. The indirect evidence that has been used in Chile to indicate the probability that a difference in supply elasticities would exist is twofold: (1) It is claimed that the percentage of land in natural pasture (which is used as an index of inefficient use of land) is directly related to the size of the farm. (2) It is further claimed that productivity per hectare is inversely related to the size of the farm. The specific studies using this evidence will be described later. Here we only point out that there is no way to test *directly* whether or not large farms would have a greater elasticity than small farms.

In addition to the type of argument used by Barroclough, another explanation for low supply response is the claim that in some Latin American countries involvement in the details of management is considered demeaning. However, even if there is such a cultural trait, there is no reason to suppose that it operates more strongly among owners of large farms than among owners of smaller farms. One might think that owners of smaller, family-sized farms, are less able to afford the luxury of such a cultural trait; but it is not uncommon for material rewards to be sacrificed even by the very poor for behavior patterns that are approved by their society. Again, the issue is empirical, and some study of differences between large and small landowners is required before it can be argued that redistribution of ownership will increase the elasticity of supply.

In addition to the question of supply elasticity for agricultural products, it is often held that a redistribution of land ownership will have another effect on development. This second effect would take place through the redistribution of income that would occur if the land were expropriated either without compensation or with compensation at less than the commercial value. If the distribution of income in a country is such that there is only limited demand for the kind of crude industrial products that a developing country can produce while at the same time demand is high for high-cost luxury products and imports, there is little opportunity for the economy to grow. An insufficient internal market for goods which might be mass-produced and an external market not easily broken into provide little incentive for investments which would lead to industrial growth.

The potential impact of a redistribution of income depends upon empirical facts and cannot be demonstrated by logic. It must first of all be true that the redistribution will take place from consumers who in fact have a low marginal propensity to consume native industrial products to those who have a high propensity. Secondly, both the industrial production functions for the goods in question and the current level of operation in these industries must be such that an increase in demand would stimulate investment in mass methods. In other words, there must be potential not only for economies of scale which are not yet reached, but also for an increase in demand of the right size which could result from an income redistribution. Before the induced investment effects of income distribution are cited as a reason for agrarian reform, evidence should be given to show that economies of scale are possible, and that the income distribution being effected is sufficiently large to cause the level of production to reach this scale.

Finally it is claimed that owners of large farms in Chile use their savings less productively than would the new owners if an agrarian reform redistributed ownership. This claim is usually made in the form of a statement about how unproductively the savings of large landowners are used. But the underlying assumption, usually unstated, must be that the savings of other possible owners would be used more productively.

The purpose of this study is to examine the validity of the two basic arguments given above as they pertain to the Chilean economy. It is specific in that the question asked is not the general one of whether the redistribution of land ownership has the effects attributed to it in these two arguments. Rather, the question is: Will the particular method by which Chile is carrying out a program of redistribution of land ownership be likely to have such effects.

This study was conducted in the following way. First, an analysis of a sample of agrarian reform farms was made to determine if more of the available land is utilized or if the land in use is producing higher yields when compared with the same farms under their former owners. Evidence that the change of ownership has led to increased output on these farms depends upon one of these characteristics being found true. A contention of increased output can only be sustained, however, if it can be shown that such an increase, if it exists, is not simply a response to prices. The study also projects the effects on agriculture as a whole which are likely to result from changes that have already occurred. This projection involves assumptions about the extent to which the law will actually be carried out and estimations of the percentage of the total agricultural sector which will be directly affected.

Second, an analysis was made of the impact of the redistribution of income likely to result from the change in land ownership. This analysis involved a study of the method of compensation to landowners, and an estimate of how much money will, in fact, be redistributed. It further involved an examination of household budgets of both the former and the new owners.

Some justification is, perhaps, required for presuming to study the effects on production and income distribution after so short a time period. One argument offered is that the Chilean government has committed itself to, and is in the process of carrying out a general restructuring of land ownership. Therefore, it is highly useful to undertake a study such as this in order to evaluate the process before it is too late to reverse or change the course of the policies should it seem advisable.

Secondly, since agrarian reform programs are being actively promoted in Latin America both by UN agencies and the Organization of American States, it is useful to analyze agrarian reforms that are already in process. The analysis can not only point out some of the issues which should be confronted in such reforms, but also present an appropriate methodology for evaluating them.

It has been argued that direct economic goals are not sought by an agrarian reform which redistributes land; that the goals are social and political. Accordingly, a study of the probable economic results is not only unnecessary but misleading.[10] There are reasons why the argument is not applicable to this study. The first is that the redistribution in Chile has continually been presented to the public, not only of Chile but of the world, as a means to improve the efficiency of agriculture. Especially noteworthy have been the constant discussions in the major Chilean newspaper *El Mercurio,* which argue that the agrarian reform either has or has not led to increases in agricultural production. The government and the Agrarian Reform Corporation have consistently defended the reform on the grounds of improved production efficiency. If these arguments are to have substance, an objective study is needed to test whether or not such improvement is actually taking place. Moreover, even if the purpose of reform were sociopolitical, they have a cost; it is useful to know what that cost is.

It is possible that those who advocate sociopolitical objectives have not considered to what extent these objectives can be accomplished in Chile through an agrarian reform. The rural population of the country is less than one-third of the total population, and it is not clear that a redistribution of income in this sector could actually effect a change in the political power structure. Furthermore, it is quite possible that the agrarian reform will actually result in a lower living standard for the urban working class. Those who argue from the base of social justice would do well to consider the implications of this possibility.

The study begins in the following chapter with a brief description of the state of agriculture in Chile. This same chapter presents and criticizes previous studies of the reasons for stagnation in this sector and the prospects for agrarian reform. In order to contribute more precise information to the discussion on agricultural supply response in Chile, this Chapter 2 also presents estimates of some of the elasticities of this sector. Chapter 3 traces the history of the legal institutions which have governed the agrarian reform in Chile. Chapter 4 is a case study of a particular farm affected by the most recent law. Chapter 5 analyzes the effect upon production within the farms involved in the agrarian reform, and projects its probable future effects on the agricultural sector. The redistribution of income which can result from the carrying out of the law is examined in Chapter 6. This analysis is followed by a study of the probable effects on both savings and the demand for domestically produced industrial products which would result from the redistribution. Chapter 7 offers a critique of various aspects of the way in which the reform is being conducted with a view toward improving the possibility of its success. Chapter 8 discusses the cost of the reform and the possible alternative measures for accomplishing the same goals. A summary of the results of the study can be found in Chapter 9.

# 2

## The Agricultural Sector in Chile

The first section of this chapter gives a brief description of the agricultural sector in Chile, within the context of the total economy, thus setting the background for the problems leading to the arguments favoring agrarian reform. In the second section, these arguments are presented and discussed. In the final section are estimations of supply elasticities in the agricultural sector.

### The State of Chilean Agriculture

The most striking feature of Chilean agriculture is its failure to produce sufficient food to meet the demands of the population. This failure cannot be attributed to the lack of sufficient land. To what can it be attributed? And, how can it be corrected?

The need of the Chilean agricultural sector to produce more food can be readily understood through a presentation of some basic facts. Between 1939 and 1964 the average annual increase in agricultural output was approximately 2.03 percent while the average annual rate of population increase has been 2.23 percent.[1] Thus, the per capita agricultural production has not even maintained itself. Even with a low income elasticity of demand for food, increase in real per capita income of about 2 percent adds further pressure on the demand for food.[a] The evidence of this pressure can be seen in the net imports of agricultural products. Before 1940 Chile was a net exporter of these products, but since that time it has each year become more of a net importer. Table 2–1 shows the index of production for the agricultural sector and the index of population growth. Table 2–2 shows the imports and exports of agricultural products.

That the agricultural failure cannot be attributed to a lack of sufficient land is less obvious but validated by the evidence. Various estimates of the amount of land in Chile which is potentially useful have indicated that land is not the limiting factor in meeting the demand for agricultural products. The criterion used most often to indicate the underutilization of land has been the large percentage of land held in unimproved natural pasture. Based on the 1955 census data various estimates have indicated that between 30 percent and 40 percent of the irrigated land in the Central Valley of Chile (the most important agricultural area as well as the area where

---

[a] The long-run real per capita growth of income for the past forty years is usually given as 1.5 to 2 percent. ODEPLAN has revised estimates of national income from 1960. The rate since that time has been in the order of 5 percent per year.

**Table 2–1**

**Index of Agricultural Production and Population (1939 = 100)**

| Year | Index of Agricultural Production | Index of Population | Index of Production per Capita |
|------|------|------|------|
| 1939 | 100.00 | 100.00 | 100.00 |
| 1940 | 97.92 | 101.70 | 96.28 |
| 1941 | 97.85 | 103.43 | 94.61 |
| 1942 | 101.55 | 104.86 | 96.84 |
| 1943 | 106.78 | 106.43 | 100.33 |
| 1944 | 113.12 | 108.13 | 104.61 |
| 1945 | 109.23 | 109.78 | 99.50 |
| 1946 | 113.81 | 111.79 | 101.81 |
| 1947 | 110.98 | 114.09 | 97.27 |
| 1948 | 114.57 | 116.40 | 98.43 |
| 1949 | 115.56 | 118.60 | 97.44 |
| 1950 | 114.30 | 121.12 | 94.37 |
| 1951 | 117.29 | 123.68 | 94.83 |
| 1952 | 115.25 | 126.63 | 91.01 |
| 1953 | 122.31 | 129.72 | 94.29 |
| 1954 | 128.14 | 132.69 | 96.57 |
| 1955 | 131.87 | 135.95 | 97.00 |
| 1956 | 134.26 | 139.59 | 96.18 |
| 1957 | 134.13 | 143.42 | 93.52 |
| 1958 | 144.39 | 147.33 | 98.00 |
| 1959 | 140.47 | 151.24 | 92.88 |
| 1960 | 146.99 | 155.22 | 94.70 |
| 1961 | 153.16 | 159.54 | 96.15 |
| 1962 | 152.74 | 163.99 | 93.14 |
| 1963 | 152.38 | 168.73 | 90.31 |
| 1964 | 163.07 | 173.54 | 93.97 |

Source: ODEPLAN.

irrigation is most important) is in natural pasture. This land could be used for either crops or artificial pasture, which would triple the number of animals that could be fed annually. The 1965 agricultural census does not distinguish between irrigated and nonirrigated land in natural pasture, but the total amount of agricultural land in natural pasture is almost 50 percent. The relevant issues of labor and/or capital restraints will be discussed later.

There are two important issues which can be raised against the argument that land is not the limiting factor in agricultural production. First, it

**Table 2–2**

**Exports and Imports of Agricultural
Products (in millions of dollars)**

| Year | Exports | Imports | Net Exports |
|------|---------|---------|-------------|
| 1936–1938 | 28.6 | 17.6 | + 11.0 |
| 1939–1941 | 20.8 | 20.1 | + 0.7 |
| 1942–1944 | 25.9 | 32.6 | − 6.7 |
| 1945–1947 | 42.9 | 55.2 | − 12.3 |
| 1948–1950 | 39.6 | 69.2 | − 29.6 |
| 1951–1953 | 42.5 | 81.7 | − 39.2 |
| 1954–1956 | 25.3 | 103.0 | − 77.7 |
| 1957–1959 | 31.7 | 83.5 | − 51.8 |
| 1960–1962 | 29.8 | 121.8 | − 92.0 |
| 1963–1965 | 29.9 | 154.3 | −124.4 |

Source: *Plan Agropecuario*, Santiago, 1966.

may be that water is a constraint on the usefulness of the available land. The complexity of the water problem in Chile is the reason for stressing the amount of *irrigated* land in natural pasture in the above discussion. If irrigation water were more efficiently utilized in Chile, still more land would be available. In the province of Coquimbo, for example, there are often complaints that abuse of water rights by some farmers prevents others from having a sufficient supply of water. But in the Central Valley, except in years of serious drought (as in 1968–1969), irrigation is seldom a problem for those who have water rights.

A second issue which can be raised is that of soil quality. It is possible that Chile simply does not have a comparative advantage in agriculture, and that farm products *should* be imported. Some observers claim, however, that the soil and climate in the Central Valley of Chile are among the best suited for agriculture in the world. Several U.S. and British farm experts compare the Central Valley more than favorably with southern California. If this is true, it is difficult to see how Chile would not have a comparative advantage in agriculture.

**The Geography**

As is well known, Chile extends from North to South in the southern hemisphere through several climatic zones. The shape of the country (the average width is only slightly over 100 miles) renders inevitable a high cost of infrastructure. The Andes Mountains on the East and the Pacific Ocean on the West make it impossible to cooperate, for example, with a neighboring country in an attempt to lower the cost of road building or electricity. There are four rather distinct agricultural zones. The northern areas are mostly desert and, with the exception of several oases, have relatively little agricultural value. The one exception is in the province of Coquimbo, which is transitional from the desert to the mediterranean climate farther south. In this area there are several large river valleys which, potentially, could serve to provide the other areas of Chile with winter vegetables and fruits. The roads connecting this area with the rest of Chile are poor, and water storage and irrigation facilities are only currently being built. The Coquimbo area now serves to provide food for local mining towns and has developed some foreign exportation of melons.

The ten provinces of the Central Valley form the single most important agricultural area. The climate is mediterranean, the soils are good. The rain comes in the winter months, so that most agriculture requires irrigated land. This area provides greater Santiago (which contains about one third of Chile's total population) with fruits, vegetables, and cereals. In addition, most of the Chilean vineyards are in this area. It has been estimated that the Central Valley contains about 39 percent of the arable land and 76 percent of the irrigated land in Chile.[2] About 45 percent of total agricultural value is produced in this area.

The frontier region, composing the five provinces to the south of the Central Valley, has sufficient rainfall during the growing season itself so that it is not so dependent on irrigation. Twenty-two percent of the value of agricultural production comes from this area. But again, as in the North, there is a serious transportation problem.

The last agricultural region is composed of the southernmost provinces. Actually, these provinces might be divided into two separate areas, one of which concentrates on forest products, the other, in the extreme south, is dominated by sheep raising. Rainfall in this region is nearly always plentiful and the climate is much colder.

Most of the present study is concerned with the Central Valley. It is to this area that most of the arguments for and against agrarian reform have referred. The typical form of tenancy in the Central Valley is owner-operated or hired manager-operated farms of very large size. Labor, for the most part, is provided by resident workers, called *inquilinos*.

### Agriculture in the Total Economy

As distinct from many other underdeveloped countries, Chile has a relatively low percentage of the labor force in agriculture. As early as 1940, the percent of the active labor force engaged in agriculture and fishing was 35 percent, and had decreased to 27.5 percent by 1960.[3] For the active male population the figures are slightly higher, falling from 43.5 percent in 1940 to 34.0 percent in 1960. The contribution to GNP has decreased from 15 percent in 1940 to 12.2 percent in 1960, and to about 10 percent in 1965.[4] It can be seen from these data that there has been a resource release in the form of labor to other sectors of the economy. This release is of dubious advantage, however, since the industrial sector was not growing fast enough to absorb the labor. For example, in December 1967, 6.4 percent of 900,000 in the work force in Santiago were unemployed, about 150,000 of these inactives would have liked to work, but had ceased to look for work.[5] Thus, pockets of unemployed workers have grown up around Santiago, the main destination of the migration. Further, for the release of labor to be a net contribution, the agricultural sector itself must continue to produce the food supply necessary for the support of the total economy. That it has not done so is evidenced by the decline in per capita food production.

As shown in Table 2–2 above, Chile has become an increasingly greater importer of agricultural products. Thus, as a provider of foreign exchange, the agricultural sector has not fulfilled one of the roles traditionally ascribed to it for developing countries. On the contrary, imports of foodstuffs have eaten up foreign exchange. There are estimates indicating that between 1950 and 1960, of the average annual imports of agricultural products of nearly $100 million, about two-thirds could have been produced from resources within Chile.[6] We are not here talking about import substitution in the sense of developing production in a particular area, but rather about expansion of production with resources which otherwise appear to have remained underutilized.

The lack of sufficient food production within Chile has put pressure, not only on foreign exchange, but also on prices of food products which are important wage goods. In order to relieve the pressure on price, the Chilean government has exercised control of the prices of various commodities since 1940. This control has been especially true of wheat, a basic necessity, which is controlled at every level from wholesale wheat sales to retail bread sales.[7] These controls have been continuously readjusted, however, and it is often argued that prices are not kept down very effectively. A comparison of agricultural products with controlled prices to products with uncontrolled prices (in both cases for products entering the general cost of living index) shows a decrease in the price of both, but a greater decrease in the prices of those products not subject to control. Table 2–3 gives these data. However, import policy which gives high tariff protection to industrial products, but not to agricultural products, vitiates the usefulness of this comparison in proving that price fixing has not really kept prices down.

One other way to transfer resources from agriculture to the other sectors of the economy should be through voluntary or compulsory contribution to capital formation from savings out of agricultural income. We will discuss in more detail later the voluntary transfer of investment funds from the agricultural sector. It appears that very little such transfer has taken place. Funds involuntarily provided, that is, taxes, have been low for this sector. In contrast to the 12 to 15 percent share in GNP between 1950

**Table 2–3**

**Index of Prices of Agricultural Products Whose Prices Are Controlled and Those Not Controlled (1951 = 100)**

| Year | Index of Prices for Controlled Products | Index of Prices for Noncontrolled Products |
|------|------|------|
| 1951 | 100 | 100 |
| 1952 | 100.7 | 113.3 |
| 1953 | 107.0 | 102.5 |
| 1954 | 111.4 | 98.1 |
| 1955 | 110.5 | 91.8 |
| 1956 | 90.0 | 87.4 |
| 1957 | 89.7 | 85.6 |
| 1958 | 92.3 | 75.4 |
| 1959 | 89.5 | 73.6 |
| 1960 | 89.1 | 86.0 |

Source: Kurt Ulrich, "La Agricultura Chilena," in *Agricultura y Tributacion*, ed Kurt Ulrich and Ricardo Lagos (Santiago: Universidad de Chile, 1965), p. 33.

and 1960, the amount of direct taxes (including property and income taxes) paid by the agricultural sector was around 6 percent of the total amount of direct taxes collected by the government.[8] The total amount of agricultural gross geographic product paid in taxes fluctuated between 3 and 5 percent in the years 1940–1962.[9] It has often been argued that taxation itself could be an incentive to the increase of farm output. Land taxes which are high induce farmers either to sell their land or to use it intensively. It could be that taxes were not high enough for incentive.

Finally, rising agricultural incomes in a developing economy are supposed to provide a growing market for an expanding industrial sector. However, this result can be achieved only if the proprietor class constitutes a large portion of the population, or if the increased incomes are shared with the farm laborers. Chile is not a land of subsistence farmers. The majority of agricultural production comes from large farms with hired labor. There is some indication that the income to farm laborers decreased between 1940 and 1955. The Institute of Economics of the University of Chile has estimated a decline of income to labor between 1940 and 1955 of about 6 percent, while farm proprietors' income increased nearly 50 percent. The share of the return to labor went from 38 percent in 1940 to about 28 percent in 1955.[10] The disparity of these figures makes them open to some question. It is quite possible that these and the shares estimated above are highly inaccurate, and that the differences are exaggerated. It is not clear how data on labor income in this sector was estimated unless it was taken as the residual. The use of social security payments would be a very inaccurate way to estimate actual wages since these are paid on the legal minimum wage, not the actual wage. The figures, therefore, are not taken as definitive evidence of declining wage share. However, it is not unreasonable that some decline took place. If there is an excess labor supply and subsistence wages are paid, the proprietor class can have received all the increase in agricultural output during this period. There is evidence that the labor supply has been overabundant. No study of farm labor has as yet been able to explain wages. This author does not think any accurate measures of farm wages are available prior to 1965. Mamalakis indicates an even more striking feature of these data by dividing labor income into wage earners and salaried employees.[11] Income to the former decreased by about 10 percent during this period while income to the latter increased by 50 percent. These figures imply that as a market for industrial products, the agricultural sector has not grown, but, in fact, may have decreased in its ability to absorb a growing supply of such products.

This study concentrates on two aspects of the agricultural sector: (1) as a provider of basic food stuffs (and other primary materials), and (2) as a potential market for industrial products. The reason for this concentration is that proposals for agrarian reform have emphasized these two aspects as their goals. The remainder of this particular chapter relates to the first of these two aspects, that of increasing the output of the agricultural sector itself.

As we stated in the introduction, it has been argued that the failure of the agricultural sector in Chile to meet the demands for food needed by the growing population is a result of the structure of land ownership in that country. Others have claimed that this is not the case, but that lack of economic incentives, resulting from government interference in the pricing system and discriminatory foreign trade regulations, has been the cause of agricultural stagnation.[12]

The case for the need of structural reform has been made especially by UN agencies and the present Chilean government. As early as 1951 the UN Department of Economic Affairs published a study called *Land Reform: Defects in Agrarian Structure as Obstacles to Economic Development*. It is interesting to note the statements made in UN documents. In 1951 the Economic and Social Council requested the Secretary-General to make periodic reports on progress in land reform. In the third report, in 1962, it is stated in the foreword that: "When linked with an agricultural revolution in the technical sense, and with supporting governmental policies as regards agricultural prices, public investment and tax incentives, needed land reforms can yield impressive agricultural development." Obviously, with all these programs going on simultaneously, it is impossible to attribute any special causality to a change in tenure arrangements. The only way the contribution of the change in tenure could be assessed is by a comparison of reform with nonreform farms when all the other programs were made available to both groups. This type of comparison was carried out in southern Italy, and there is evidence that very favorable results occurred in areas where land reform was implemented. (Unfortunately, however, no study has attempted to separate, *within* the area, those farms which have and those which have not changed ownership in the land reform program. Thus it is still impossible to tell whether the land reform itself is the cause of or a contribution to substantial increased productivity, or whether it is simply a result of the other programs.)

In the fourth report, in 1965, one of the stated assumptions was that "there is now such a widespread acceptance of the view that land tenure arrangements should be deliberately readjusted in order to promote economic and social development."

In none of these documents, however, is there a systematic attempt made to test the hypothesis that there is a relationship between structure and productivity.

Almost any discussion of the reform by the Agrarian Reform Corporation of Chile (hereafter known as CORA) or by government officials has included such statements as the following: "The badly managed agriculture is insufficient to supply us with the food we need and obliges us to import large quantities of food from abroad. It has been calculated that in the single year of 1964 Chile lost through bad management in the agricultural sector $120 million." [13] And it is always implied that redistribution of the land to those who work it will alleviate this problem.

By 1960, money from the Alliance for Progress was made contingent on the initiation of agrarian reform in the recipient country. It has been argued that such reform was necessary for economic development, that it was a necessary means to achieve an increase in agricultural production. It is true that other arguments of a social-economic nature were also given. But the power of an argument which implies that land will be better utilized if the structure of ownership is changed cannot be underestimated in a country where food imports are high while land resources are underutilized. Further, the major emphasis in current publications defending the agrarian reform in Chile has been placed on changes in productivity claimed to have resulted from the reform. For example, in a speech on May 22, 1967, President Frei said:

In the Province of Santiago alone, data show that at the moment of expropriation, only 38.9% of the irrigated area was cultivated, leaving 61% in natural pastures. These same farms, one year after having been made *asentamientos,* worked by the peasants have increased the percentage of land cultivated from 38% to 76.4%, and decreased the irrigated land in natural pastures from 61% to 23%. In general, in the *asentamientos* the income generated has more than doubled.

In spite of these statements, there is very little evidence of either cross-country or within country correlations between agricultural productivity and the structure of ownership. Some early attempts were made from the data furnished by the 1955 agricultural census in Chile to investigate the relationship between the size of land holding and the output of the farm, but when account was taken of land quality there was no clear relationship between these two variables in Chile.[14]

The evidence that has accumulated in favor of the argument that the structure of ownership is the cause of the stagnation in agriculture in Chile has been compiled and analyzed by CIDA (earlier mentioned as a committee formed jointly by various UN organizations, the Interamerican Development Bank, and the Organization of American States). Its purpose was to study the characteristics of land tenure in various Latin American countries, and to study the relationship between agrarian reform and agricultural development. In 1966 the committee published its report on Chile: *Tenancia de la Tierra y Desarrollo Socio-Economica del Sector Agricola.* The preface of this study states that the principal hypothesis is

. . . . that the systems of land tenure now existing in Latin America, predominantly the "latinfundia" and "minifundia," can be modified to achieve a more rapid economic and social development. A corollary of this hypothesis is that the present systems frequently constitute an obstacle to development. Concretely, it is believed that an intelligent reform of the actual systems of tenure, destined to redistribute the rights and benefits of property to those who work it, can . . . lead to a considerable increase in the agricultural productivity, thanks to the better use of land, labor, and other agricultural resources.

### The Structure of the Tenancy

It is not difficult to show that land ownership is highly concentrated among very few owners in Chile. Table 2–4 shows this distribution from 1955 census data. Approximately the same distribution would hold using 1965 census data, but, since the arguments in the CIDA report all refer to the 1955 data, we use this year also in order to be consistent.

The classifications in this table were devised by CIDA, but no fixed amount of land is indicated in their definitions. Regardless of the exact definitions, it is clear that 23 percent of the farms contain 92 percent of the total area and 90 percent of the irrigated area. Because many large landholders own more than one farm the concentration of ownership units is greater than the concentration of operational units. The most common organization on the multifamily-sized farms is that of a large number of so-called "obligated workers" who live in company housing and work on the farm as needed. Either the owner or the hired administrator plans and allocates the jobs to be done. Additional laborers are hired as needed from

**Table 2–4**

**Number and Area of Farms According to Size Group**

| | Less Than Family Size [a] | | Family Size | | Multifamily Medium Size | | Multifamily Large Size | |
|---|---|---|---|---|---|---|---|---|
| | Number | Percent | Number | Percent | Number | Percent | Number | Percent |
| Number of farms [b] | 55.8 | 37.0 | 60.4 | 40.0 | 24.4 | 16.1 | 10.4 | 6.9 |
| Total area [c] | 78.1 | 0.3 | 1966.2 | 7.1 | 3149.9 | 11.4 | 22518.1 | 81.2 |
| Agricultural area | 67.4 | 0.3 | 1762.8 | 8.1 | 2823.0 | 13.1 | 16983.9 | 78.5 |
| Arable area | 57.5 | 1.0 | 642.6 | 11.6 | 1220.3 | 22.0 | 3623.0 | 65.4 |
| Irrigated area | 23.6 | 2.1 | 80.0 | 7.3 | 138.4 | 12.6 | 855.9 | 78.0 |

Source: The CIDA report, p. 43.

[a] The CIDA report defines these categories loosely. *Less than family size* are those farms which are not large enough to provide a family with the basic necessities. *Family size* is that amount of land which is sufficient to provide a family with a "satisfactory level of living," and can provide enough work for the family group. *Multifamily medium size* are farms which require hired labor outside the family group, but do not require a complicated hierarchical structure of organization. The *multifamily large size* farms are those which require a hierarchical organization for their adequate and competent functioning.

[b] Thousands of units.

[c] Thousands of hectares.

outside the farm. The source of this labor is either owners of small plots of land or migrant workers with no land. Seventy percent of the farms in Chile are either directly or indirectly owner operated. The remaining 30 percent of the farms is rented for a fixed sum, worked by sharecroppers, or used by workers in partial payment for labor.

## The Structure of Ownership and Productivity

The general outline followed by the argument presented in the CIDA report is the following: the efficiency of land use, measured by the percentage of available land actually cultivated and measured by the value of output per hectare, is inversely correlated with the size of farms. Furthermore, larger farms have greater access to credit and to markets than do small farms. Thus the greater value per hectare on small farms occurs in spite of, and not because of, market and credit facilities. The evidence that these statements are true, CIDA argues, supports the hypothesis that the owner of the small farms have more incentive to produce than do the owners of large farms. In order to show that this relationship between size and efficiency is, in fact, a causal one and not simply coincidental, other possible explanations of low output in the agricultural sector are examined. CIDA

**Table 2–5**

**Use of Arable Land According to Size of Farm as a Percentage of Land Held in Each Stratum**

| Group | Annual Crops | Fallow | Fruits and Vineyards | Artificial Pasture | Natural Pasture |
|---|---|---|---|---|---|
| Less than family size | 38.5 | 6.1 | 21.4 | 4.7 | 29.2 |
| Family size | 26.3 | 12.7 | 5.6 | 3.0 | 52.3 |
| Multifamily medium size | 21.9 | 12.5 | 3.5 | 6.0 | 56.1 |
| Multifamily large size | 23.2 | 11.8 | 2.4 | 10.8 | 51.7 |

Source: The CIDA report, p. 147.

argues that neither pricing policy nor foreign trade policy can explain the low output.

The evidence given for the first part of the argument, that the percentage of land owned that is cultivated is inversely correlated with the size of the farm, is shown in Tables 2–5 and 2–6. (Cultivated land equals land in annual crops, land in fruits and vineyards, and land in artificial pasture.) It is not at all clear from these tables, that there is an inverse relation between size of farm and idle land, as the CIDA would claim. (Land in natural pasture is not, strictly speaking, idle. It is often used as pasture, but because no attempt is made to improve its usefulness as pasture nor to

**Table 2–6**

**Use of Irrigated Land According to Size of Farm as a Percentage of Irrigated Land in Each Stratum**

| Group | Annual Crops | Fallow | Fruits and Vineyards | Artificial Pasture | Natural Pasture |
|---|---|---|---|---|---|
| Less than family size | 39.1 | 13.1 | 37.9 | 9.9 | — |
| Family size | 38.3 | 6.7 | 18.6 | 6.0 | 30.4 |
| Multifamily medium size | 28.7 | 5.3 | 10.6 | 13.0 | 42.4 |
| Multifamily large size | 39.5 | 2.2 | 7.4 | 23.1 | 27.8 |

Source: The CIDA report, p. 148.

cultivate it, we use the term "idle" here.) What is clear from the census data is that land-holding units of less than family size cultivate a larger percentage of their land than do farms larger than this. But tables 5 and 6 show that the largest farms actually cultivate a larger percentage of land than do family-sized farms. It is difficult to see, therefore, how this evidence can be used to support the hypothesis that larger farms use land less intensively than smaller farms. The advocates of agrarian reform seek the creation of family-sized units, not units of less than family size.

CIDA has estimated the value of production per arable hectare to show that this value is inversely correlated with farm size. Table 2–7 shows the results of their calculations.

There is no data given, however, on the differences in land quality. It is impossible to know from the CIDA data whether or not the smaller properties are indeed more efficient. Results of the air-photograph study made of the land surface of Chile in 1961 do not give evidence that the smaller farms have better land on the average than larger farms. A report by the

**Table 2–7**

**Estimate of the Value of Agricultural Production According to Size of Farm**

| Group | Value of Output (E° 1,000's of 1960) | Arable Surface (1000 Hectares) | Value of Output per Arable Hectare (E°'s) |
|---|---|---|---|
| Less than family size | 22,500 | 57.5 | 391 |
| Family size | 81,098 | 642.6 | 126 |
| Multifamily medium size | 177,111 | 1220.3 | 96 |
| Multifamily large size | 299,817 | 3623.0 | 83 |

Source: The CIDA report, p. 150.

Institute of Research on Natural Resources in 1967 gave the fiscal value of land per arable hectare for farms in the stratum from 0.1 hectare to 50 hectares as about equal to that for farms over 500 hectares.[15] Farms between 50 and 100 hectares were slightly more valuable per arable hectare than those larger and smaller. Although these facts do not prove that the land quality on smaller farms is not significantly better than the land quality on larger farms, they do support such an interpretation, since, according to law, the fiscal value is based on potential productivity. We do have, then, one strong piece of evidence that land is used more intensively on smaller farms than on larger farms. The CIDA report does not specify the manner in which their calculations on value of output per hectare were made, there is therefore no way of criticizing their validity. Furthermore, what is of significance to the economy is net output and not gross output, and no account has been taken of costs in these calculations.

After giving the above evidence to support the hypothesis that small landowners use land more intensively than large landowners, the CIDA report argues that credit channels are more open and markets more accessible to large landowners. The estimates made on credit availability by size of

**Table 2–8**

**Distribution of Credit by Size of Holding**

| Group | Percentage of Producers | Percent of Arable Surface | Percent of Credit Received | Percent of Value of Output |
|---|---|---|---|---|
| Family size and smaller | 76.9 | 21.1 | 7.0 | 39.8 |
| Multifamily size medium and large | 23.1 | 78.9 | 93.0 | 60.2 |

Source: The CIDA report, p. 178.

farm are generalized from an analysis of two of the various credit sources available to farmers. Credit from these two sources constitutes about 33 percent of all farm credit. There is reason to believe that these sources are biased in favor of the small landowner relative to other credit sources and would, therefore, overestimate the total credit going to small landholders. Based on this evidence CIDA estimates the distribution of credit as shown in Table 2–8.

In addition to the inaccuracy that may have resulted from generalizing about only two of the credit sources, there is some underestimate of the credit actually available in the first group of Table 2–8. In this particular estimate, CIDA has included sharecroppers and those resident laborers who receive the use of an area of land as partial payment. It is known that a wide variety of relationships exist between these workers and the owners of the farms involved. In some cases, seed is provided; in other cases, tools are loaned. In addition, it is known that owners often lend money to these laborers. No study has been made on the interest rates charged in these cases, so it is not possible to evaluate the credit given in this way. The point is that there is an unknown amount of credit which occurs outside the banking system. If this group of borrowers were eliminated from the table, there would still be a disproportionate amount of credit in the upper bracket relative to both the percent of land held and the value of output, but the figures would not appear as skewed as they now do.

No actual data are given on access to markets by size of farm. It is simply argued by CIDA that small farmers are at a greater disadvantage because they concentrate on horticultural crops in which the marketing and storage facilities are relatively poor. There is some contradiction in the CIDA argument here. First, the following data are given: participation in the final sales by intermediaries in beef went from 57.5 to 60 percent between the periods 1952–1956 and 1959–1963; in wheat they went from 57.9 to 63.9 percent between 1950 and 1960. CIDA then argues that since the large landowners concentrate in these products, they have suffered less from marketing difficulties because "in the sale of wheat and beef there are no marketing problems since internal production does not cover the needs of the population." [16] But surely the increase in the percentage share by intermediaries reflects some sort of market problem.

These are the basic data used in one way or another by those who argue that the structure of ownership is the cause of the low level of production in the agricultural sector. Authors making this argument have usually included data on relative prices compared to indexes of output to indicate that there is no reason to believe that price policy can explain the low level of output. The same data on price and output have been used by others to show that the price policies do explain the behavior of farmers. Table 2–9 shows the historical relation of wholesale prices in agriculture to wholesale prices in the industrial sector.

It is evident from this table that the price controls put on certain agricultural products in 1940 did not work to depress relative agricultural prices. Relative prices after 1940 are, in general, higher than before 1940. With the exception of the 1952–1955 period, when they were high, these prices have not changed very much. Putting an index of output next to the price index tells us nothing without a theory of price response for farmers; and, in any case, the indexes give us no estimate of how strongly farmers actually do respond.

Those who have argued that government policies have held down incentives for farmers generally discuss the price policy, compare Chilean prices with foreign prices, and discuss commercial policy; but there has been no effort to present a systematic argument using data covering a number of years which could explain the low level of farm output on the basis of traditional profit maximizing behavior. A typical case of the sort of argu-

**Table 2–9**

**Index of Agricultural Prices Relative
to Industrial Prices (1955 = 100)**

| Year | Index of Relative Prices | Year | Index of Relative Prices |
|------|------|------|------|
| 1928 | 70.4 | 1945 | 78.0 |
| 1929 | 75.3 | 1946 | 78.2 |
| 1930 | 67.5 | 1947 | 84.3 |
| 1931 | 53.0 | 1948 | 84.4 |
| 1932 | 61.5 | 1949 | 84.8 |
| 1933 | 61.6 | 1950 | 86.4 |
| 1934 | 62.0 | 1951 | 87.7 |
| 1935 | 64.7 | 1952 | 98.3 |
| 1936 | 67.8 | 1953 | 98.4 |
| 1937 | 71.2 | 1954 | 105.6 |
| 1938 | 69.1 | 1955 | 100.0 |
| 1939 | 69.1 | 1956 | 88.0 |
| 1940 | 75.8 | 1957 | 90.2 |
| 1941 | 84.7 | 1958 | 75.3 |
| 1942 | 80.6 | 1959 | 75.5 |
| 1943 | 83.5 | 1960 | 87.1 |
| 1944 | 80.8 | 1961 | 86.8 |

Source: Eduardo Garcia, "Inflation in
Chile" (Ph.D. thesis, Department of Economics, MIT, 1965), Appendix, Table II.

ment used is found in Mamalakis.[17] He shows that the commercial poultry
business and broilers tripled between 1944 and 1954, and that sugar-beet
production tripled in four years. Both these products were given special
governmental incentives. He presents a table of price and output indexes,
and argues that they show output to be price responsive. He then states:

> These are a few among the many instances that present a picture of a group
> of farmers who are "backward" when penalized, overtaxed, oppressed, or
> exploited and "progressive" when rewarded, protected and helped. They re-
> spond and follow financial incentives with the fluctuations in wheat output being
> a perfect example of this behavior. No reason appears to exist why agriculture
> could not duplicate the spectacular gains of Chilean industry if treated, sub-
> sidized, and protected in similar fashion.[18]

**Test of Supply Responsiveness**

In an attempt to contribute more precise information about the sensitivity
of the Chilean agricultural sector to ordinary incentives, one part of this
study is devoted to an estimate of the response of these farms to price

changes. As stated above, what is needed in Chile is more of everything and not simply more of one crop in relation to another. One could argue that if farmers responded strongly and quickly to a relative price change between two or more products they would, indeed, be behaving as profit maximizers, and would respond to normal financial incentives to expand total output if such incentives were forthcoming. There is a certain logical fallacy in the transition from arguing that farmers respond quickly to relative prices in the allocation of a given piece of land to a particular crop to arguing that farmers will respond as quickly to financial incentives to expand total land planted or to increase yields on all crops by the addition of fertilizers. In other words, it does not follow that a high supply elasticity for a given crop will imply high supply elasticity for all crops taken together. In the following section we make two kinds of estimates. The first estimate tests the responsiveness of area planted in wheat to the relative price of wheat. The second estimate tests the responsiveness of area planted in all crops to changes in the prices of agricultural relative to industrial products.

For the first type of estimate, that for an individual crop, wheat was chosen because of its importance in total agricultural production and because of its treatment by the government price policies. It has been one of the most carefully controlled prices because of its importance as a wage good. Imports of wheat have been large since 1950. The need, therefore, to be able to get more wheat on the market without too large an increase in price is apparent. There has been a considerable amount of variability, not only in the price of wheat in absolute terms, but also in its price relative to other agricultural products. We can, therefore, estimate the supply price responsiveness using data on area planted in wheat by province as well as the area planted for all of Chile. Estimates of supply elasticities were made for five separate provinces in Chile as well as for Chile as a whole. As in the case of total acreage for all crops, both the absolute price and the relative price of wheat were tried. To what is the relative price relative? Ideally, we would want some price index of all crops which might compete with wheat for the use of resources. It was assumed that the best index for this purpose was the index of prices for all nonlivestock agricultural products. This choice is clearly arbitrary for two reasons. Some of the land cannot be easily used for wheat. In addition, some of the resources devoted to livestock could, in fact, be transferred to wheat. The issue is further complicated by the fact that the price of wheat itself is part of the index for all nonlivestock products. However, since it is not a large part of this index, it was felt that the usefulness of this index would not be unduly impaired. The only other alternative would have been to construct an index of all major competing crops. The gain in accuracy from constructing such an index however, was not sufficient to justify the time involved.

For the second estimate there are serious conceptual as well as practical problems. The main conceptual problem is determination of those specific prices to which farmers should be expected to respond. If we assume that the index of agricultural prices relative to the index of industrial prices measures the relative profitability of the two sectors, then if farmers are truly profit maximizers they will respond to more favorable relative prices by expanding production. The trouble with this argument is that it assumes that farm owners have a given amount of capital to invest and are simply looking for the most profitable opportunities for investment. But in the Chilean case it is claimed that farm owners having high incomes already, simply are not interested in maximizing profits. Because the marginal utility of the extra income from expanding output is rather low, it would take a large increase in profits from agriculture to induce the large land-owners to put forth the extra energy required to expand total output. If this is the case, farm owners may respond to increases in absolute agricultural prices, but not to agricultural prices relative to industrial prices. We shall test both cases in order to see which price seems to be the more relevant. The relative prices will test the argument that agriculture has not progressed because it has been less profitable than industry and farm owners have, therefore, invested in the industrial sector. The use of absolute prices will test the argument that farm owners are only concerned with their sector and require large increases in prices to expand their output.

The model used to measure the supply responsiveness is that presented by Nerlove [19] and elaborated by Behrman [20] with adjustments made for the particular situation in Chile. Inasmuch as the criticisms of the assumptions of this model were amply discussed by Behrman, they will not here be repeated. Only a brief enumeration of the assumptions and their relevance to the Chilean case will be given.

The model assumes that a close approximation to the elasticity of the responsiveness of planned agricultural output to the expected price for that output can be obtained by the estimation of the responsiveness of planned acreage to the expected price. This assumption implies that the elasticity of planned yield with respect to expected price is negligible. To the extent that this elasticity is not negligible, the elasticity measured by the model is underestimated. Planned output, then, is expressed as a function of expected price and other variables which may affect it in addition to price. Behrman incorporated not only the expected price, but also as a risk factor, the variance of prices over a recent period. In addition, he used expected yield and the variance of the yield over the recent past. In the case of Chile, because most agricultural output is not produced by subsistent farmers, but rather by large landholders, risk was not considered such an important element. Therefore price variance need not be used. Furthermore in the model tested here the expected yield is considered to be the actual yield. The decision to use actual yield was based on the assumption that Chilean farmers have fairly accurate control over the yield. This is true because in the Central Valley and in the North, the planting season follows the rainy season and thus farmers know how much water will be available for irrigation. The amount and timing of water is usually one of the most important causes of unplanned changes in yield in agricultural production. In the south of Chile, such dependence on rainfall during the growing season is important, but this area is relatively less significant in the production of crops.

The following formulation of the model is the result of the adaptation of the Nerlove model to the Chilean case.

$$A^d = a_{11} + a_{12}P^e_t + a_{13}Y_t + a_{14}R_t + u_{1,t} \tag{1}$$

where

$A^d$ = the desired area to be planted in period $t$
$P^e_t$ = the expected price in period $t$
$Y_t$ = the yield in period $t$
$R_t$ = rainfall in period $t$
$U_t$ = the error term

Desired area is related to the actual area in the form of an adjustment mechanism.

$$A_t = a_{21} + A_{t-1} + a_{22}(A^d_t - A_{t-1}) + u_{2,t} \tag{2}$$

This equation says that the actual area planted in period $t$ is equal to the actual area planted in the previous period plus some fraction (or all if $a_{22} = 1$) of the difference between the desired area of this period and the actual area planted in the previous period. In other words, it is presumed that, for a given crop, the change in the area planted, $A_t - A_{t-1}$, is probably not equal to the difference between the area desired in time $t$ and the actual area in the previous period, but rather to some portion of that difference. One important reason that this fraction will not be 1 is that rotational schemes may present some restraint on just how much area can be planted in a certain crop in a given year. This constraint may also imply an adjustment coefficient of greater than 1. Finally, the expected price is related to the actual price.

$$P^e_t = a_{31} + P^e_{t-1} + a_{32}(P_{t-1} - P^e_{t-1}) + u_{3,t} \tag{3}$$

This model is then manipulated to get an expression of the actual area planted as a function of observable present and/or past variables.

$$\begin{aligned} A_t = &\, a_{12}a_{22}a_{31} + a_{32}(a_{21} + a_{11}a_{22}) + [(1 - a_{22}) + (1 - a_{32})]A_{t-1} \\ &- (1 - a_{22})(1 - a_{32})A_{t-2} + a_{12}a_{22}a_{32}P_{t-1} + a_{13}a_{22}Y_t \\ &- a_{13}a_{22}(1 - a_{32})Y_{t-1} + a_{14}a_{22}R_{t-1} - a_{14}a_{22}(1 - a_{32})R_{t-2} \\ &+ a_{22}u_t - a_{22}(1 - a_{32})u_{t-1} \end{aligned} \tag{4}$$

Several problems present themselves in the estimation of this model. One problem is that ordinary least squares would be inefficient since there is not a unique way to recover the individual $a_{ij}$'s. This problem is overcome by assuming values for $a_{32}$ and varying this value over a range between 0 and 2. The value which gives the minimum standard error of the regression is then chosen. The equation is rearranged in the following way in order to obtain unique values for all $a_{ij}$'s by linear estimation.

$$
\begin{aligned}
A_t - (1 - a_{32})A_{t-1} = {} & a_{12}a_{22}a_{31} + a_{32}(a_{21} + a_{11}a_{22}) \\
& + (1 - a_{22})[A_{t-1} - (1 - a_{32})A_{t-2}] \\
& + a_{12}a_{22}a_{32}P_{t-1} + a_{13}a_{22}[Y_t - (1 - a_{32})Y_{t-1}] \qquad (5) \\
& + a_{14}a_{22}[R_t - (1 - a_{32})R_{t-1}] \\
& + a_{22}[u_t - (1 - a_{32})u_{t-1}]
\end{aligned}
$$

The second problem is the unlikely probability that the error term in the equation actually estimated is not serially uncorrelated. This is a problem that occurs in all models with a distributed lag. If the original form of the equation has a lagged dependent variable, it is not so likely to have serially uncorrelated error terms. But when the lagged dependent variable is a result of algebraic manipulation of a distributed lag, then the probability that the errors are serially uncorrelated is decreased. Such a coincidence would demand that the error terms in the original equation have the same specific lag structure as that appearing in the final equation. If the original error terms are uncorrelated, then the error terms in the lagged form cannot be uncorrelated.[21] In order to attack the problem, the Hildreth–Lu technique to estimate the lag structure of the disturbance terms was used,[22] with the standard errors adjusted for the presence of a lagged dependent variable.[23]

We turn now to the results of the model as it is applied to wheat. Tests were made for five of the twenty provinces for which there is data on wheat acreage. In two of these provinces, wheat is relatively more important, both as a crop among crops in the province and as a percentage of the total amount of wheat produced. Table 2–10 shows the coefficients of the reduced equation for both the five provinces and for Chile as a whole.

In three of the five provinces and for Chile as a whole, the coefficients of

**Table 2–10**

**Coefficients of Reduced Equation for Wheat in Five Provinces and for Chile as a Whole**

| Province | Constant Term | Price | Yield | Rainfall | Lagged Area | $\bar{R}^2$ |
|---|---|---|---|---|---|---|
| Chile | −834.8 | 255.9 | 227.2 | −0.017 | 0.933 | 0.86 |
| | (227.7) | (44.95) | (5.1) | (0.35) | (0.094) | |
| Coquimbo | −13 | 18.4 | −0.18 | 0.053 | 0.218 | 0.78 |
| | (1217) | (5.7) | (0.34) | (0.017) | (0.195) | |
| Santiago | 38.2 | 11.5 | −0.67 | 0.002 | 0.289 | 0.73 |
| | (127.8) | (13.2) | (0.29) | (0.008) | (0.199) | |
| Colchagua | 11.4 | 9.03 | 0.45 | −0.008 | 0.904 | 0.90 |
| | (16.4) | (8.3) | (0.60) | (0.006) | (0.223) | |
| O'Higgins | 15.7 | 32.7 | 0.66 | 0.016 | 0.350 | 0.55 |
| | (18.9) | (7.9) | (0.33) | (0.006) | (0.157) | |
| Cautin | −17.7 | 84.4 | 1.45 | −0.02 | 0.48 | 0.58 |
| | (75.6) | (23.9) | (1.79) | (0.16) | (0.21) | |

the price variable are significant. The implied price elasticity at the means in each case is shown in Table 2–11.

When the wheat price is deflated by the cost of living index rather than by the price index for other agricultural products, only one province has a significant price coefficient. The implied elasticity in this case is 0.48. (The province here is Colchagua which is not one of the three with a significant price coefficient.) The implied elasticity for total area with respect to price is 2.36 with 10 percent of the adjustment again made in the first year.

**Table 2–11**

**Elasticity of Desired Area Planted with Respect to Expected Price**

| Province | Elasticity | Percent of Adjustment in the First Year |
|----------|-----------|------------------------------------------|
| Coquimbo | 0.92 | 80 |
| O'Higgins | 2.0 | 65 |
| Cautin | 1.2 | 42 |
| All Chile | 3.65 | 10 |

*Note:* It will be recalled that the coefficient of $P_{t-1}$ in the reduced equation is not itself $a_{12}$, but rather $a_{12}a_{22}$. The coefficient of the lagged area variable is $(1 - a_{22})$. Thus $a_{12}$ is calculated by subtracting the coefficient of the area variable from 1, and dividing the price coefficient by the result. The elasticity at the mean is then calculated from $a_{12}$. This is the elasticity of desired area planted with respect to expected price. The actual adjustment in a given year is found from the area adjustment coefficient, $a_{22}$.

The short-run price elasticities implied here for total wheat acreage are 0.36 for relative price and 0.23 for the absolute wheat price. It is interesting that a simple model which was tried gave very similar results. This model assumed that desired area planted was equal to actual area planted, and that the expected price in period $t$ was equal to the actual price in period $t - 1$. It expressed area planted as a function of price and an index of rainfall. The price coefficient, but not the rainfall coefficient, was significant. The implied elasticities were 0.30 for the relative price index and 0.18 for the absolute price index.

If these results are accepted as reasonably accurate, we can then argue that the long-run price elasticity for area of wheat with respect to the expected price of wheat (either relative to other agricultural prices or in absolute terms) is strong, but that the time needed for the actual area planted to reach the desired area is rather long. If we measure the amount of additional wheat actually needed in Chile by the imports of wheat we can estimate that an increase of 25 percent is required. In order to say what change in price could effect an increase of 25 percent in the quantity of wheat produced, we need to know whether or not the price elasticity of the yield is indeed negligible. A test was made on wheat yields using the simple model:

$$Y_t = a + bP_t + cR_t + u_t$$

where $P$ is the price of wheat and $R$ is the rainfall index. Both relative prices and absolute prices were tried as well as prices for period $t - 1$. In no case was there a significant price coefficient. Therefore, we take the elasticity of area planted to be equivalent to the elasticity of quantity. In order to achieve a 25 percent increase in the quantity of wheat, a sustained increase of either 6.8 percent in the relative price of wheat or a 10 percent increase in the absolute price of wheat would be required. (These two values are not entirely independent since the price of industrial products enters into the cost of living index that is used to deflate the money price of wheat.)

In spite of these positive results, it is still not clear what would happen to the rest of agriculture if the price of wheat were allowed to rise. If the wheat acreage were simply to be expanded at the expense of some other crop or crops, then the imports might simply change from wheat to other crops. This, however, may be regarded as an improvement, depending on the other crop. If some less necessary products were cut back, their imports could be held down through trade policy. But even though an increase in wheat production relative to other crops may be an improvement from the production point of view, there is still the question of the effect of price increase for wheat on the cost of living. If the price elasticities of demand for wheat are low, the equilibrium price might in fact rise significantly if price controls were removed and import policy on wheat were changed. Again, we are faced with the issue of the optimum price and whether or not this equilibrium price could not be lower if land ownership were different.

We now examine the response of total acreage to prices in order to evaluate the effect on other crops of an increase in wheat acreage.

For total acreage there is no indication of a significant positive price elasticity. In the full model, the coefficients of equation (5) are given below.

$$
\begin{aligned}
A_t - (1 - a_{32})A_{t-1} = \ & 76.04 + 0.042\,(a_{32})P_{t-1} \\
& (53.74) \quad (0.092) \\
& + 0.232\,[Y_t - (1 - a_{32})Y_{t-1}] \\
& \quad (0.108) \\
& + 0.048\,[R_t - (1 - a_{32})R_{t-1}] \\
& \quad (0.032) \\
& + 0.129\,[A_{t-1} - (1 - a_{32})A_{t-2}] \qquad \bar{R}^2 = 0.74 \\
& \quad (0.388)
\end{aligned}
$$

The only coefficient which is significant is that on yield. The price used in this equation was the index of agricultural relative to industrial prices. When real agricultural prices alone were used, the price coefficient is significant, but negative. The following results were obtained in the latter case.

$$A_t - (1 - a_{32})A_{t-1} = 169.3 - 0.27(a_{32})P_{t-1}$$
$$(16.6) \quad (0.07)$$
$$- \ 0.215[Y_t - (1 - a_{32})Y_{t-1}]$$
$$(0.085)$$
$$+ \ 0.0518[R_t - (1 - a_{32})R_{t-1}]$$
$$(0.0196)$$
$$- \ 0.0366[A_t - (1 - a_{32})A_{t-2}] \qquad \bar{R}^2 = 0.84$$
$$(0.024)$$

In both cases above, the value of $a_{32}$ which gave the smallest standard error of the regression was equal to 1.5.

It is difficult to interpret the negative price coefficient. Taken together, the two results above would seem to indicate that the relative price does not influence the desired area and that the absolute price of agricultural products is inversely related to the desired area. An attempt to use a more simple model based on the assumptions that actual price was anticipated with a large degree of accuracy and that the desired acreage was equal to the actual acreage, gave no better results. The price variable was again insignificant. If it were true that Chilean farmers responded in a negative way to the expected price of products, we would then argue that they do not behave as profit maximizers in the traditional sense, but rather with some income goal in mind; and thus, when prices get relatively high, they work relatively less. This behavior is not inconsistent with even a high supply elasticity for an individual crop, since switching from one crop to another is not as troublesome as extending the entire area planted. If there is a definite income objective, a farmer might concentrate on the most profitable crops to meet this goal and still not be willing to extend his entire operation.

Before letting this interpretation stand, it is important to point out the possible flaws in the model. One reason this model may be misspecified for total acreage considerations is its failure to account for input prices.[b] When testing the response of a particular crop to its relative price, it is reasonable to assume that input prices are not an important consideration, since the cost of most inputs would be the same regardless of what crop they were used for. But, when testing the response of all acreage to an index of prices for all agricultural products, input prices do matter. However,

[b] This same problem occurred in an attempt to estimate the responsiveness of fertilizers to relative output prices. Various types of models were tried both for all fertilizers and for all specific kinds of fertilizers. No relationship was found between these variables and output prices. However, the model is clearly unspecified without fertilizer prices and these were not available.

changes in input prices could only explain the negative price coefficient if an index of output relative to input prices moved in the opposite direction to the index of output prices alone. Such a negative relation is seen to exist only for the three years 1952–1954. It should be noted, however, that data on input prices, available from 1946 (see Appendix B), are of doubtful validity, inasmuch as a large part of the input prices are labor costs, and it is extremely difficult to know these costs because a large portion of them is paid in kind.

Another flaw in the model is the failure to consider the possible reaction of farmers to the fact that political, rather than market considerations may govern price fixing policies of the government. This interference and its unreliability may make farmers unresponsive to price movements. However, this still cannot explain a negative relationship between area planted and absolute price.

A third possible misspecification may be the use of industrial prices as the deflator in the relative price index. Capital gains on foreign exchange or on land may be alternatives to investment in farming. The policies required to get more agricultural production when such alternative profit opportunities exist and are operative, are quite different from the policies required when the major alternative is investment in industry.

Finally, the model fails to consider other variables which may have affected the profitability of farming during this period. An example of such a variable is credit availability. There is no evidence for the period under consideration that credit policy toward agriculture has changed significantly. In particular, there is no evidence that credit policy toward agriculture relative to credit policy toward industry has changed.[24]

The purpose of this section has been, not to prove or disprove the contention that price policy is the cause of agricultural stagnation, but rather to show the kind of analysis that is needed before the issue can be discussed with confidence. Such analysis should have occurred before productivity arguments were used to justify a program of agrarian reform. The cost to the economy as well as the implications for income distribution between the rural and urban workers could have been analyzed for alternative programs. Furthermore, even if an agrarian reform were to be carried out for frankly other than productivity reasons, the price elasticities of various levels of farm size should have been estimated since it is still necessary to know whether or not the output from agriculture will be improved, decreased, or stay the same when the same price policies are continued. These estimates would be possible if data collected in the annual sample study of acreage use and production were presented according to farm size and not simply by province. There is not enough difference among provinces in tenure systems and land ownership concentration to be able to conclude anything about their relative behavior from studying elasticities among provinces. If there were significant differences of land concentration among provinces, some interpretation of the different elasticities for wheat in different provinces might have been given. For example, the province of Cautin does have a larger proportion of sharecroppers than do other provinces, while, on the other hand, the three provinces of Santiago, Colchagua, and O'Higgins are very similar to each other in tenancy characteristics. The fact that Cautin and O'Higgins were the two provinces with high supply elasticities allows us no interpretation which relates tenancy to size of elasticity.

The division of land into family-sized farms raises a still more serious issue for industrial growth. What is of prime concern for such growth is the elasticity of supply of the marketable agricultural surplus, and not that of actual production. It is reasonable to expect that for large landowners, whose income elasticity of food would be low, the difference between the price elasticity of supply for production and for the marketable surplus would not be great. This may not hold for the owners of family-sized farms.

Careful studies along the lines of this chapter were not made prior to the decision to redistribute ownership of land in Chile. Therefore, this study does not further examine the issues raised here, but rather analyzes the results that can be expected from the reform already in process. It is hoped that such a projection, by putting into relief the ramifications of certain policies, contributes toward an understanding of what may be expected from land redistribution as a tool for overall economic development. The analysis begins with a history of the legal institutions established in Chile to implement this redistribution.

# 3     History of the Legal Institutions for Agrarian Reform

The early history of Chile is similar to that of other Latin American countries. The Spanish crown granted large tracts of land as rewards or favors to individuals. Although the intent of the crown was for the individual to be overseer in its name, or organizer of an area to protect and educate the native population, these individuals regarded themselves as owners and acted as such. From this system developed the particular distribution of the large amount of land held in the hands of a small percentage of the population. Until the 1800s the large landowners were not only the strongest economic power of Chile, but also the strongest political power. After the war with Peru and Bolivia in 1879, when Chile obtained land with large mineral resources, the growth of a middle class of industrialists and miners led to the gradual decline of the political power of landlords. This decline interacted with a simultaneous liberal movement in Chile designed to improve the conditions of the poor, grant freedom of religious belief, expand educational facilities, and reform the political structure.

It is not surprising, then, that in 1925 a new constitution was approved in Chile. The new constitution made specific reference to the fact that the right of property is "subject to the limitation imposed by the need to maintain and improve the social order." This limitation is much broader than that placed on property ownership in the earlier constitution (1833), which simply recognized the right of eminent domain for the state. The 1925 constitution made it possible for the *Caja de Colonizacion Agricola* to be formed. The law establishing this organization was part of the general reform movement to improve the working conditions, income levels, and living conditions of the less privileged classes in the society. To this end, the *Caja* was empowered to colonize state lands and to buy land belonging to private individuals for the purpose of dividing it into smaller units and selling it on favorable terms to new owners. Although the objective of the *Caja,* as stated in the law, was to create a better distribution of the land, it was not given the power to expropriate land. It is possible, however, that had its funds been sufficient, its power to buy and subdivide land could have significantly changed the structure of landholding in Chile. The *Caja* was intended to be a largely self-financing venture, although both its budget and the payments required of the beneficiaries were expressed in nominal values. From as early as 1890, Chile suffered from the chronic inflation which has characterized her history. The consequent declining real value of *Caja*'s funds left it with little capacity to function. In general, the procedure of the *Caja* was first, to purchase a farm; second, to carry out studies with the purpose of projecting the income level possible given soil quality, etc.; and third, to divide the farm into "economic units," or parcels. Each economic unit was supposed to be of a size capable of providing a living for the family group. Until 1960, the level of income implied by "living" was not defined. The apparent intent was to provide enough land to occupy the family workers, but not so much that other laborers would need to be hired. If, for technical reasons, some part of the land should not be divided, it could be larger than one economic unit. This larger area was called a *lote*. It could be sold to an individual under the same conditions as the parcels, sold at public auction, or sold to a cooperative of owners of parcels to use together. In the 30 years between 1929 and 1960, the *Caja* established 94 colonies in which 3,392 families had either parcels or *lotes*. The annual rate of formation was about 110 per year. The entire number of families settled represented about 1 percent of Chile's families in agriculture in 1960.[1]

There were no established criteria for the selection of new owners. Consequently, political factors, among others, often influenced the selection. In many cases persons with no agricultural experience or training were granted parcels. The subdivision of lands often displaced former resident farm laborers, for these were not given primary consideration. For this reason a new law in 1960 established a third type of subdivision called a *huerto,* which was equivalent to a house and garden plot but not large enough to satisfy the needs of a basic subsistence living. The *huerto* was granted to the former resident laborers of a farm.

This same 1960 law established a point system for the selection of new owners; and, although its criteria made the granting of land depend on agricultural experience, it favored those who had previously been administrators or had served in some other position of responsibility.

In the entire process of the *Caja*'s operations, the parcels formed were generally larger than could be worked by an individual man. What actually developed was a system of operation similar to that of the larger farms. The new owner became the administrator, and he hired labor to work his farm. In many cases the resident labor system was adopted on these farms as well. Thus, even though the size of farms might be changed, the social system of tenancy was not affected. In a case study made by CIDA only three of the thirty-four new owners of a particular farm were chosen from the resident labor force of the farm. The remaining *inquilinos* received *huertos* and provided paid labor for the owners of the new parcels.

During the three years between January 1960, and December 1962, 420 families received parcels, and 527 workers received garden plots. If we consider only parcels, the annual rate of formation was slightly higher in this second period—140 against 110 on the average per year in the earlier period.

In November 1962, the *Caja* was changed to the Corporation of Agrarian Reform, or CORA. In the law that made this change, Law #15020, CORA was given the right to expropriate private property under certain conditions.

Article 30 of this law declared that its purpose was to carry out an agrarian reform such that those who worked the land should have access to its ownership. The other objectives stated in Article 30 were that the standards of living of agricultural workers be improved and that agricultural production be increased. Article 30 changed the policy regarding the receivers of the land. In the earlier law, definite favor was given to already experienced persons who had held a position of responsibility. This new law favored the granting of land to those unskilled workers who were either resident laborers or migrant workers. The objective of increased agricultural production indicates the growing sentiment that the structure of the landholding in Chile was an obstacle to agricultural efficiency. This sentiment was expressed in the conditions of expropriation which the law allowed. Land could be expropriated if it were badly managed or abandoned. Given the large amount of land in this category in Chile, it was believed that expropriating this land and selling it to the persons who now worked on it would lead to improved agricultural production. This assumption implied that the land, when distributed to those who worked it, would no longer be badly managed. In addition to lands that were managed inefficiently, properties held by juridical persons who did not operate them directly (for example, Church-held lands which were rented) were subject to expropriation.

Under the 1962 law, CORA was to pay for the land in cash. The constitution was amended in the following year to allow deferred payment for properties "abandoned or manifestly badly managed." These deferred payments were to be adjusted each year according to the rate of inflation. The recipients, although given a period of grace, were to pay for the land under much the same conditions. The allowance for deferred payment made it possible for CORA to expropriate more lands than had been possible under the law of direct cash payments. In practice, though not in theory, lands expropriated under this new law were compensated at full commercial value. This practice resulted from both court interpretations and the desire of CORA to avoid a court fight.

The 1962 law also required that property owned by state agencies such as the National Health Service be sold to CORA. This provision made it possible for CORA to begin operation with a large number of farms, without either political complications or prolonged cases in the law courts. Between November 1962 and November 1964, CORA distributed land to 1,066 families in the form of 781 parcels and 285 garden plots.

Apart from the government-instituted agrarian reform program, a voluntary program was also initiated in 1962, and implemented on 3,000 hectares of Church-owned property in the dioceses of Santiago and Talca. This program was begun before the 1962 law was passed, but many have thought it was influenced by the expectation of the passage of the law since under it the Church lands would have been expropriable. This particular transfer of property was carried out under the auspices of the *Instituto de Promocion Agraria,* or INPROA, which was able to obtain financial assistance from the Interamerican Development Bank. In an attempt to circumvent the problem of lack of management training which is often anticipated in the redistribution of land to workers, INPROA developed a system which has come to be called "gradualistic turnover." [2] This system involved a transfer of land from the former owner to a cooperative formed by the new owners with technical assistance given by INPROA. During the first two years the farms were operated as a single economic unit by the members of the cooperative. In the third year divisions into parcels were made, and not until the fourth year were individual land titles given. Results of this particular reform will be discussed in a later chapter.

When the government of Eduardo Frei was elected in 1964 on a platform of a more effective agrarian reform, CORA was reorganized along lines similar to INPROA. It was decided that in the future a similar method of gradualistic turnover would be used in the government expropriations. In fact, the leadership of CORA was turned over to the former head of INPROA. Although the law requiring this form of transfer was not passed until 1967, the actual program was begun almost immediately on the assumption of office by the new administration in January 1965. During the period of investigation for this study, all farms were still in the cooperative ownership stage. While in this period, the farm is called an *asentamiento*. Because this study concentrates on what has occurred in *asentamientos,* it is relevant to spell out in detail the objectives established in the law for this organizational structure.

In Article #66 of Law #16640, the period of the *asentamiento* is described as "the transitory step in the social and economic organization of the farm workers; in which the lands expropriated by the Corporation of Agrarian Reform are cultivated until such lands are definitively transferred" to their new owners. The principle objectives of the *asentamiento* stage as stated in the law are the following:

1. To cultivate the lands efficiently, improving their production through the assistance of CORA;
2. To train the members (the future beneficiaries) for the responsibility of being farm managers;
3. To develop a community and promote cooperatives in it; and urge them to use most of their income for investment;
4. To construct the infrastructure necessary for the development of community living and for the normal cultivation of the farm.

The following chapter describes an individual *asentamiento* in detail in order to make clear exactly how it functions.

There are several aspects of Law #16640 which provided for a more thorough restructuring of the pattern of ownership than had hitherto been possible. The first of these is stated in Article #3, which made expropriable all agricultural lands "of the same owner, wherever be its location in the national territory . . . that either in part or in total, has an extension of more than 80 standard hectares of irrigated land," calculated according to a conversion table. The conversion table is an attempt to equalize the production possibilities of the nonexpropriable land. It contains a table of equivalents for each zone and type of land that established, for example, how much dry, hilly land would be equivalent to 80 standard hectares of irrigated land. The standard unit is not necessarily land of the best quality since it was possible in some areas to have less than 80 actual hectares equal to 80 standard hectares. There is a certain amount of inevitable arbitrariness in the table, however, inasmuch as land in the same general geographic area is not necessarily of uniform quality. For example, in the province of Santiago, one hectare of irrigated land "suitable for the crops of the zone" is equal to one hectare of standard irrigated land. One hectare of irrigated land "with serious physical limitations for the crops" of the zone is equivalent to 0.47 hectares of a standard unit. It is true that there were special areas within the Santiago province which were converted separately, but even so, it is quite possible that two farms quite close to each other may not have equally good soil. The decision of whether or not the soil had "serious physical difficulties" was made by an agricultural engineer on first visiting the farm for CORA.

Also expropriable were lands which were found abandoned or badly managed regardless of size. This provision is the same as that of the earlier law, although it was not to be applied to properties of less than 80 standard hectares until 3 years from the time of the promulgation of the new law.

A badly managed farm is defined in the law (Article #1) as a farm whose cultivation takes place under "inadequate economic, technical or social conditions." These conditions are not set forth in the law itself except insofar as a minimum set of criteria is given. This set demands that at least 80 percent of the useful area of normally irrigated land be in annual crops, permanent crops, or artificial pasture. In the case of land not normally irrigated, at least 70 percent of the area must be in crops or at least in improved natural pasture. Also specifically stated as bad management is the judicial conviction of infractions against laws regulating minimum wages, social security payments, and the dismissal of workers. This particular aspect of the law is of great concern to many land owners at the present time. Because of the clause "inadequate social conditions," there is some fear that workers will deliberately instigate strikes for the sole purpose of creating a situation which could result in the expropriation of the property. One of the properties used in this study was in fact expropriated because of a prolonged strike. And in some interviews unrelated to this study, the author was told by landowners that anyone seen visiting the home of a resident laborer would be immediately approached and questioned by the owner, who reserved the right to expel him from the property. In other words, because the worker lives in a house owned by the landowner himself, the latter feels justified in controlling who does and who does not visit these persons, at least in their houses. It might be mentioned here that the CORA officials react the same way on the *asentamiento*. One must obtain permission from the zonal office of CORA to visit and talk to members of *asentamientos*. Professor Edel has questioned whether this practice itself might be challenged under the law as "inadequate social conditions," but, up to the present time, no one has challenged it. And, as the practice is also common on the *asentamientos,* it is doubtful that it will be so challenged.

Since CORA has the right to expropriate lands under Article #3 on the basis of size alone, it might be asked why there would be concern over the clause on bad management. For farms of less than 80 hectares, there will be no problem until 1970. However, farmers can be concerned that during this time the workers will begin to organize, and that, as soon as possible, they will start to agitate in such a way as to force expropriation. For farms of over 80 hectares, there is a very important issue at stake here. As will be seen later when discussing indemnification, there is a different payment procedure depending on the reason for expropriation. If the "condition" is bad management, the terms of payment to the former owner are very much worse than if expropriation is based on size alone. This particular problem is mitigated somewhat, however, by the fact that it is more time-consuming for CORA to face the legal battles that often ensue when the condition of bad management is used. In fact, CORA's own internal decision in mid-1968 was to use the condition of size alone for future expropriations even though it is more costly in money terms.

Some families divided their land among several sons and daughters in lots of 80 hectares during the 2 years the law was in the legislature. In order to prevent this practice from being an escape from expropriation, the size limit was made retroactive to November 1964, the year of the election. In addition, lands which even before that date were legally but not operationally divided in the agricultural year immediately following the legal division, were not exempt from expropriation. Thus any property of greater than 80 standard hectares either legally or operationally as of November 1964, was subject to expropriation.

Persons whose land is expropriated under Article #3 have the right to a reserve of 80 standard hectares. But if the condition of expropriation is bad management there is no right of reserve. Although the reserve is selected by the owner, its location is subject to certain limitations. The area must be contiguous, it must contain proportionally the quality of land which in fact exists in the entire farm, and it must not inhibit the rational use of the water rights in the rest of the farm. These, and other limitaions, make it impossible for the reserve to hamper in any way the operation of the expropriated lands or to contain in itself only or all of the best quality of land in the farm.

There is some protection in the law for two groups of farm owners. For persons who run an extraordinarily well-managed farm, Article #21 sets up conditions that give them the right to hold as much as 320 standard hectares:

1. The farm must have at least 95% of the irrigated land in crops or artificial pasture and 80% of the nonirrigated land in crops or improved pasture.
2. The Minister of Agriculture must certify that the property is cultivated "in conditions of productivity superior to those predominating in the same region for equal quality land."
3. The Minister of Agriculture must also certify that soil and other natural resources are kept in a good state of conservation.
4. The employees must participate in some form of profit sharing, the percentage of gross output to be determined by the President of the Republic.
5. Workers must be paid at least twice the minimum daily wage and have an annual income of at least twice the "sueldo vital" of the zone.ª Housing and other noncash payments cannot account for more than 15% of these payments.
6. No serious violation of social legislation or labor legislation within the last two years can have occurred on the farm.

Probably the most cutting of these conditions is number five. Although it is not at all unusual in Chile to find permanent workers paid twice the minimum wage, it is unusual that this is paid in cash.

The second group exempted from the law of expropriation consists of vineyard owners. This exemption, too, has many qualifications. In addition to the conditions established for the exemption of well-managed farms in the six points above, the exempt wine industry (1) must have a capital investment of at least four times the value of the land itself; (2) must have at least 95% of the vineyard in varieties and qualities approved by the Minister of Agriculture; (3) must commercialize at least 50% of the normal production in good quality wine; and, (4) must have at least 10% of the shares of its stock in the hands of the employees of the farm.

These qualifications for exemptions make it quite clear that the law has exempted very few farms from possible expropriation.

Compensation for expropriation is paid partly in cash and partly in bonds. The farm is evaluated at the amount currently used as the basis for tax payments. Tax assessments, according to law, are based on the potential

---

ª "Sueldo vital" is a yearly sum considered a minimum annual income in which a worker can live. It is also the basis of measurement for income tax payments and certain kinds of other tax payments. Since this sum is adjusted each year according to a cost of living index, it allows a unit of measurement which is not so variable as the inflationary nominal values.

productivity value of the farm. However, the tax assessment values are generally regarded as being below the current market values.[3]

There are three classes of payment established in the law. These classes depend for their application on the condition of expropriation. For land expropriated on the condition of size beyond 80 standard hectares, owners are paid 10% of the payment in cash and 90% in class A bonds. These bonds are paid in 25 equal annual installments. Each installment is divided into two parts: 70% of each payment is adjusted according to the cost of living index and 30% is not adjusted at all. The interest rate is 3% which is paid on the face value of the 30% part and on the face value adjusted by 50% of the cost of living index on the 70% part. The interest rate, on the 70% part, is effectively 2½ percent on the basis of a 20% inflation rate; less with a higher rate of inflation. Interest on the nonadjusted part is equal to −17% with an inflation rate of 20%.

Owners of lands which were abandoned are paid 1% in cash and the rest in class C bonds. The only difference between these and class A bonds is the length of time required for payment. Class C bonds are paid off in 30 annual installments rather than 25.

Owners whose lands are expropriated under Article #3 and who make use of their right of reserve receive only 1% of the value in cash if the reserve is equal in value to the 10% cash they would otherwise receive.

As regards indemnification, then, the implications of the 1967 law are quite different from those of the 1962 law. The earlier law resulted in payment on the commerical value of the farm. The new law requires payment of approximately 73% of the fiscal value. The remaining 27% is ignored because an average inflation of at least 20% per year would soon wipe it out. Sixty-three percent of the total is paid an interest rate of approximately 2½% when the rate of interest on risk-free capital is in the order of 5%. For lands judged badly managed the payment is less. This procedure shows that the law has compromised between confiscation and expropriation with full payment. This fact affects the discussion of whether or not income is redistributed. If full payment is made by the recipients of the land, there may be a temporary redistribution of income among the recipients and some other sector of the economy during the period of grace usually given before payments begin. But when this is not the case there is no redistribution from owner to worker. Only if the landowner receives partial payment for the land, as in the case of the 1967 law, is there any possibility of redistribution from the landowner to the worker.

# 4

## Case Study of an Individual *Asentamiento*

In order to clarify terminology and also to give a clear idea of just how an *asentamiento* functions, this chapter presents in detail a description of a particular *asentamiento*.

The universe of this study is the set of 53 *asentamientos* formed prior to August 1, 1966 between the provinces of Coquimo and Nuble. The purpose of selecting this date was to ensure one year of experience prior to the study. Strictly speaking, May 1 is the beginning of the agricultural year. However, because a large number of *asentamientos* was formed between May and August, and because it was felt that for these *asentamientos* the major planting decisions would have been made after August, it was decided to include them in the universe. A random sample of 20 from among the 53 *asentamientos* was selected. This sample was originally chosen by the Instituto de Capacitacion y Investigacion de Reform Agraria (ICIRA), which had been commissioned by CORA to make a study on the viability of the *asentamiento*. The author worked directly with the ICIRA team in the collection of production data.

For most of the analyses of this study only 17 of the 20 *asentamientos* selected could be used. In one of the three exceptions the accounts were not yet audited and therefore not available as of April 1968. The other two were likewise eliminated because of lack of information. This lack of information is significant in the light of later considerations. The members of these two *asentamientos* were able to circumvent CORA in the sale of output and therefore did not repay CORA for any of the advances made during the year. CORA records for these farms thus contained only costs and advances, but no income. The *asentados* were not willing to give information, and, in fact, claimed that production was negligible.

The *asentamiento* chosen for the case study here is one of the most smoothly operating of the seventeen. The reason for this choice is to indicate the ideal situation. Various deviations from this norm will be pointed out.

### The Asentamiento Prior to Expropriation

Before being expropriated, this farm of 850 hectares, of which 560 are irrigated, was owned by a single individual. Forty-five families lived on the farm in houses belonging to the owner. The family head of this type of resident laborer in Chile is called an *inquilino*. The laborer is obligated to work as needed by the owner. He is free to leave, but may not be removed by the owner without serious reason subject to legal hearing. In addition to this legal control of eviction, Chilean law protects the *inquilino* in various other ways. He cannot be required to work more than eight hours a day and he must be given off for legal holidays. He is paid by the day and his wage is subject to a minimum wage law. (These laws have existed since 1950.) There is little evidence in recent years of violations either of the eviction code or of wage regulations. Neither is there evidence that *inquilinos* have been prevented from leaving on the basis of a debt obligation. It is conceivable that the treatment of *inquilinos* has improved as a result of fear of expropriation; but there is no way of knowing this since there exist practically no studies about *inquilinos* before 1962 when the first agrarian reform law was passed.

The wages paid the *inquilinos* were in cash and kind. Cash payments on this farm expressed in escudos of 1967 were 3.56 for a day's work. (The 1967 exchange rate was approximately E°5 per $.) Payment in kind included the following: use of a house; a garden plot of about ¾ hectare; use of about 1.2 hectares of land in the regular crop rotation of the farm; the right of pasture for two animals; ¼ kilogram of uncooked beans and two large buns for each day of work. It is typical on such farms that slightly higher wages are paid for jobs which require more responsibility. There was no way to obtain information on the exact spread of wages according to the levels of responsibility prior to expropriation.

In addition to *inquilinos,* this farm, as well as others, hires nonresident laborers. These may be permanent in the sense that they work on the same farm for nine to twelve months of the year, or they may be temporary in that they are hired for only a few months. These workers, coming from outside the farm, are called *afuerinos.* Typically they are paid slightly more in cash wages, but they receive no land, housing, or grazing rights.

In mid-1965, CORA officials visited this farm to investigate whether or not it might be expropriated. The following statement was made regarding the then current use of the farm: "there are no crops nor even animals except about 16 horses." According to this report the land was used in the following pattern:

> 160 hectares of artificial pasture
> 116 hectares fallow
> 557 hectares in natural pasture

The remaining land was reported to be in infrastructure and roads. The CORA report listed 26 *inquilino* houses, all but 4 of which were in a bad state of repair. A barn with a capacity for 150–200 cows was being used to house 4 families.

On the basis of the CORA report, the farm was judged badly managed and was expropriated in October 1965. According to the CORA data, the value of the land for tax purposes in 1965 was E°76,000. However, the final settlement in 1966 for the land plus the value of improvements and infrastructure was given at E°1,177,073. The payment of the land was to be in 25 annual installments at 4 percent interest. The principal and interest were to be adjusted each year according to the index of the cost of living.

### Asentamiento Organization

Between October 1965, and June 1966, the farm was in the period of what is called pre-*asentamiento*. During this time it was run as a state farm. It was managed by a CORA official and instruction was given at meetings of *inquilinos on* how the agrarian reform would function in relation to them. CORA social workers held meetings with the women of the farm to instruct them on the agrarian reform and to organize a women's club for the purpose of gaining competence in sewing, nutritional standards, or any other aspect of a woman's life that might be of interest. Before signing the contract making this farm an *asentamiento* in June, the *inquilinos* voted in a committee of five from among themselves who, together with two representatives of CORA, formed the administrative committee to take charge of managing the farm for the year 1966–1967. Every year of the *asentamiento* a new committee will be elected by the former *inquilinos,* now called *asentados.*

The agrarian reform law requires that each farm be governed in this way for at least three years with the possibility of extension of two additional years. At the end of this time, the land titles are to be given to the *asentados.* It is up to CORA to decide whether or not the *asentados* are sufficiently prepared to close the *asentamiento* period at the end of three years.

The titles to the land can be given to the *asentados* in either of two ways. They can be given to the individual heads of families on land which will be parceled. Or they may be given to a group of families on land which will continue to operate as a single unit farmed by several families. The choice of method is legally the prerogative of the *asentados* themselves.

Of the two CORA officials who are members of the administrative committee, one lives on the *asentamiento* with his family. His job is to give technical advice as it is needed by the *asentados.* CORA insists that this person, called the coordinator, is not to run the farm. However, there are large differences from one *asentamiento* to another on just how this job is interpreted. In the *asentamiento* singled out here, the coordinator is a young man in his late twenties who has the title of what in Chile is called a "tecnico agricolo." This basically means someone trained in practical agriculture. This particular young man was exceptional in many ways. He told of several cases in which he had presented ideas of improvements in methods of planting or dairy management. In order to teach by experience rather than by dictation, he suggested experiments in which his plan was carried out on one piece of land or with one cow, and the *asentados'* plan was carried out on another. In this way the *asentados* were persuaded by their own eyes, and they gained confidence in their coordinator's knowledge. In addition, the *asentados* are gaining knowledge of a simple scientific methodology which they themselves can find useful in the future.

**Asentamiento Production**

The land in this *asentamiento* is farmed as a unit, that is, the plan of rotation for the entire farm (with the exception of garden plots of one hectare surrounding each *asentado* house) is determined by the administrative committee. Work is assigned to individual *asentados* on a daily basis depending on what is to be done. This same committee also acts as the supervisory personnel. The organization of the farm work, therefore, is seen to be similar to that which existed under the former owner. The main decisions are made, however, by a committee instead of by the former owner or manager.

**Table 4–1**

**Land Use for 1966–1967**

| Crops | Hectares |
| --- | --- |
| Wheat | 90 |
| Oats with clover | 142 |
| Beans | 51 |
| Corn | 140 |
| Sunflower (for oil) | 43 |
| Tobacco (an experiment) | 1.5 |
| Potatoes | 12 |
| Sugar beets | 36 |
| Fruit trees | 3 |
| Artificial pasture | 119 |
| Natural pasture | 150 |
| Garden plots | 44 |
| Infrastructure | 15.5 |
| Total: | 847 |

Source: *Asentamiento* records.

During the first year of the *asentamiento,* the land was used as shown in Table 4–1. In addition to crops, the farm operated a dairy. The stock for this dairy, 90 young heifers, was provided by CORA. This stock, together with 23 work animals and 155 male calves for fattening, constitutes part of the capital investment of CORA which is supposed to be paid back by the *asentados.* Payment of this capital is not required to begin until after a three year grace period following the *asentamiento* stage. Livestock and machinery are to be paid off in five years after the grace period. All other capital invested by CORA is to be paid back over a period of thirty years under the same conditions of adjustment for inflation with which the bonds paid to the owner are treated.

## Asentamiento Accounting

During the agricultural year all inputs were bought through the zonal office of CORA on credit and charged to the account of this *asentamiento*. In addition to providing this credit CORA advanced E°115,206 in cash to individual *asentados* on the basis of the number of days worked by each. An advance of E°8.5 was made for each day worked. The family allowance of approximately E°17 per month for each dependent was paid to the *asentados* and charged to general expenses.[2] This amounted to E°25,384 additional income to the *asentados*. The advances of the 44 *asentados* for the year 1966–1967 thus amount to E°140,690 which is an average of E°3,424. In addition, each *asentado* had a garden plot of one hectare which he cultivated almost entirely for consumption. Some individuals own animals with which they may have augmented their incomes. In November of 1967, after the accounts of the *asentamiento* were audited, each *asentado* received his share of the profits less the amount he had received during the year in advances. In the future the *asentamiento* will instead pay into the social security administration and the family allowance will be paid from this government agency. A problem of the legal status of *asentados* led to some confusion regarding this allowance. Strictly speaking, the *asentados* are no longer employed workers and the family allowance system should not apply. However, due to the pressure from *asentados,* the Agrarian Reform Law of July 1967 modified the former regulations of this system. *Asentados* are treated now by the agency as employed and the *asentamiento* as employer. In the interim between 1965 and 1967, many, but not all *asentamientos* paid the entire family allowance out of general expenses.

In the accounts of all *asentamientos,* income is equal to sales, inventory, changes, crops not yet harvested, and valuation of increased weight of animals grown for sale as meat. (These animals belong to CORA. They are, as it were, given to the charge of an *asentamiento* which is credited with the *increase* in value as measured by increase in weight of the animals.) Costs equal direct costs of production including payments to workers not *asentados,* and general expenses. No charge is made for depreciation. On this particular *asentamiento* CORA had not provided any machinery. Therefore, all machine costs were rentals which would, of course, be expected to include depreciation costs. For infrastructure and livestock no allowance was made for depreciation. The difference between the income and costs as described here is the profits to be divided between CORA and the *asentamiento*. The figures for the *asentamiento* under study here are as follows:

| | |
|---|---:|
| Income | E°762,466.09 |
| Expenses | 517,028.29 |
| Profits | 245,437.80 |
| CORA's share 15% | 36,815.67 |
| *Asentamiento* share | 208,622.13 |
| Subtract advances | 115,206.05 |
| To be distributed | 93,416.08 |

CORA makes no charge for interest on the advances made to *asentados* nor on the credit given for inputs. The 15 percent of the "profits" which went to CORA in this case would not be sufficient to cover even a nominal interest rate of 20 percent on the circulating capital. This rate would merely maintain the real value of the capital in question. CORA estimates total administrative costs per *asentamiento* at approximately 2 percent of the total debt of that particular *asentamiento*. In this case, total debt to CORA including that for livestock and tools is equal to E°1,501,349. CORA's share of profits is just slightly over 2 percent of this value.

Since working capital is provided to CORA from the central government's budget, the failure on the part of CORA to charge interest and the failure of CORA's share of the "profits" to cover this interest imply that there has occurred a subsidy from the central government to the *asentados*. The subsidy is equal to the difference between the alternative real interest rate which would have accrued if the money had been invested differently and the $-20$ percent real interest rate actually received. Part of this subsidy would have occurred in any case between the rest of the economy and the farm owner, because the interest rate charged for circulating capital from the Banco del Estado would have been around 18 percent, which would not have covered the inflation rate. This subsidy implies not a redistribution of income from the landowners to *asentados,* but rather a redistribution from all other sectors to *asentados*. There is a further redistribution of the latter kind. CORA has also made the land payments for this year and will continue to do so until after three years beyond the time the title is conferred. During this time all income beyond that which would be considered payment for labor is a subsidy from the rest of the economy. Estimates of the return to capital will be made in a later chapter. We turn now to the actual payments that were made to *asentados*.

The total amount of cash income received directly from the *asentamiento,* as distinct from income received from the garden plots and private capital, is summarized here:

| | |
|---:|---|
| E°115,206 | in advances |
| 25,384 | in family allowances |
| 93,416 | in the share of final "profits" |
| E°234,006 | Total received |

Of the amount due in profits, E°93,416 at the end of the year, E°4,000 were used to purchase shares in community capital. This is equivalent to a payment to CORA for the livestock and tools loaned by that agency. An additional E°9,150 was used by individuals to purchase from CORA animals for their own private capital. The subtraction of both these figures from the E°93,416 profits to be distributed leaves E°80,266 which was simply paid out in cash to the 44 *asentados*. The amount each one received was determined by the number of days he worked during the year.

The total share of *asentamiento* income divided by the number of *asentados* gives an average of E°5,318 per year. This is not the total income of *asentados*. Additional income is earned on private capital (mostly animals), through the use of a house, garden plots (mostly consumed directly—not sold), and grazing rights for animals. On this particular *asentamiento,* garden plots were estimated to have provided a net income of E°57,400, and income from livestock was estimated at E°79,200. Both of these figures include the income to the capital and labor of the individual *asentado*. The addition of these figures to cash income gives an average of E°8,198. This is still an underestimate in view of the failure to account for the use of a house and for grazing rights. At the official exchange rate, this figure is equal to approximately $1,626. It can be compared with an estimate made in 1965 for *inquilinos* in two nearby provinces of $1,108.[5] A further comparison can be made with an estimate made in 1966 for the large fundos in the entire Central Valley of $1,242.[6] This latter figure is gross income without deductions for costs on garden plots or other costs of operation. These costs are usually small for *inquilinos,* so the 1965 and 1966 estimates are probably about the same. They include estimations of the value of housing, grazing rights, and other payments in kind such as firewood, which were omitted in the estimate for the *asentamiento*. So we see that the income of an *asentado* is considerably above that received by a typical *inquilino*. It must be recalled, however, that this income is the income not only to labor, but also to capital, which at this time is still the property of CORA.

On some *asentamientos* the share of profits to go to *asentados* less the amount paid out in advances is negative. On others the amount paid out in advances is greater than total profits including CORA's share. The treatment of these negative amounts by CORA has led to problems in the concept of income later used to estimate a cross-section consumption function. Strictly speaking, the income of the *asentados* should be equal to their share of the actual profits plus the family allowance. Any amount received in advances beyond this should be treated not as income, but as an increase in debt. However, the evidence suggests that *asentados* treat the advances as wages and make no comparisons between the probable income of the farming operation and the amount being advanced. There is no correlation between consumption and the strict definition of income. Although CORA emphasizes that the advances are merely loans and must be paid off out of the profits at the end of the year, CORA does not make clear what will happen if profits do not cover the amount of these loans. At the present time, these balances are merely carried forward in the books to the next year, and there is no interest charge nor adjustment for inflation. In one case among the *asentamientos* studied, the amount paid out in advances was equal to four times the value of the actual profits. *Asentados* interviewed were aware of a debt to CORA, but were not clear as to how the debt would be paid. The issue is further complicated by the fact that the accounts are not audited until at least six months and in some cases up to a year after the end of the agricultural year. Thus *asentados* do not know whether they will owe money or will receive money in addition to the advances until they are well into the next agricultural year. In this study, then, positive and negative year-end balances are treated asymmetrically in the estimation of a consumption function. Positive amounts are counted as disposable income. Negative balances are ignored. Disposable income is equal to the advances received during the year from CORA, the income from private operations of garden plots or livestock production, family allowances, and profits distributed after the accounts are audited (these were counted as income for the year in which they were received).

# 5 Production on *Asentamientos*

In order to discuss the effect of the Chilean agrarian reform on the present agricultural production, we must separate three aspects of the problem. First, what, if any, have been the changes in production on the *asentamientos* in the sample studied? Second, can these results be generalized to all the *asentamientos* in operation in 1967? Third, what is the effect of the agrarian reform on the production of farms not expropriated?

In order to make any projections on the future of agricultural production, two further questions must be asked. Can the results on the *asentamientos* now in operation be expected to be the same as those which will occur in future *asentamientos*? This question must be raised since all the *asentamientos* in existence in January 1968, were formed from farms expropriated under the law prior to July 1967. It will be recalled that the condition for expropriation under the earlier law was "bad management." On the other hand, the law of July 1967 allows expropriation on the basis of size alone. It is possible, therefore, that the *asentamientos* in the study sample constitute a different universe from that of *asentamientos* to be formed in the future. In this case no specific projections can be made, though it still may be possible to indicate the effect on the projections these differences would have.

The second question concerns the assumption that the transition from *asentamiento* to titled ownership will not cause any major changes in production. This is a shaky assumption, posited on the belief that CORA has given and will continue to give a high priority to production and will not bestow titled ownership until it is certain that production can at least be maintained. If CORA does not operate in this way, but simply allows the three year period of *asentamiento* to be followed by a free choice on the part of members as to what they will do, two alternatives become possible. The *asentados,* once given complete control, may, in fact, be motivated more highly than before: in this case an increase in production would result. On the other hand, once actually given title to the land, the *asentados* may return to the original, or an even less efficient, way of managing the farm. In principle, CORA could control the latter possibility by supervising credit and reconfiscating farms when land and house payments are not made. However, this latter course seems highly improbable since the political climate in Chile will not readily accept such a solution. What at this moment seems most likely is that CORA will maintain vigilance over the farms over the next three years, at least, and will not allow any decreases in production. We, therefore, would expect that with regard to any *asentamientos* now in existence, any increases in production due to better land use and any increases in productivity per hectare will be maintained.

We then proceed to a discussion and estimation of the effect on production within the *asentamientos* of the sample studied. In principle, the data needed here concern the use of land, inputs, and outputs of the *asentamientos* both in the year of the study and the year prior to expropriation. With allowances made for random effects of weather or other variables, it would be possible to give accurate measures of productivity per hectare and per labor unit both before and after the *asentamiento* was formed.

An alternative estimate of the change in production could be obtained in a cross-section study. This approach would involve the selection of a sample of similar farms. It would have the advantage that the same prices of inputs and outputs would have prevailed for both the *asentamientos* and the private farms. However, a cross section would have the disadvantage that the process of agrarian reform may very well have affected non-expropriated farms—and this effect may be either adverse or favorable.

After the passage of the first agrarian reform law in 1962, there are two different, but apparently rational responses farm owners may have had. If there had been a very strong desire to hold on to the farm, together with hope that slightly better management would decrease the chances of expropriation, a farmer may well have initiated at least some types of improvement in the management of his farm. In general, since the criterion for "bad management" has usually been the existence of a large percent of idle land, a farmer might merely begin to cultivate a larger proportion of his land. On the other hand, if the farmer believed there was little hope of retaining the land, he may very well have become even less interested in cultivating the farm. Either of these effects would prejudice the comparison of *asentamientos* with other farms. In any case, in the present political climate, it is extremely difficult to obtain interviews with farmers who may have reason to fear expropriation. Any visitor is highly suspect, and if it is known that the information desired has anything to do with the agrarian reform, however remote, landowners simply refuse to talk. The reliability of any information they did give would, under these circumstances, be open to question.

### Pre-Asentamiento Data

The big problem, then, for a before and after comparison, lies in obtaining data for present *asentamientos* before they were expropriated. There are two sources for such data. The first is that obtained from CORA. CORA had to demonstrate, before a farm could be expropriated, that it was being badly managed. (This condition did not apply, of course, to farms offered for sale to CORA or to the National Health Service farms, which were automatically sold to CORA.) In addition to the data needed to demonstrate bad management, adequate data was also needed to project farm costs and income for CORA in the future. Thus, before expropriation, CORA officials (trained agricultural engineers) visited the farms, obtained information on the amount, types, and current use of land available; the physical facilities; and the potential labor force. Unfortunately, until late 1967, no consistent set of data was obtained for each farm. It is possible to make quite detailed comparisons for some farms, but few or none for others. In very few cases was actual production for any year ever obtained in this visit of CORA officials; so, although comparisons of land use can be made to an extent, almost nothing can be said about production itself on the basis of CORA data.

The other source of detailed data for most prereform farms is in the Agricultural Census Bureau for farms expropriated after June 1965. Since the majority of the farms now in *asentamientos* were expropriated after that time, the Census Bureau in fact does possess data on these farms. This census was made between April 20 and June 20 of 1965 on all farms in Chile. It was not based on a random sample, but rather was collected from every person who cultivated even a small parcel of land. Even this source, however, does not have information on all inputs; so, although output comparisons are in principle possible, output per unit of input comparisons are not. Output comparisons themselves are limited to certain crops. On other crops the census collected only acreage and not production. Since the 1965 census data are used in the comparisons of this study, a short description of the problems connected with the use of this data is in order.

**Census Data**

The Agricultural Census of 1965 was the fourth such census in Chile's history. The census immediately prior was made in 1955. This fourth census was originally scheduled for 1960, but the severe earthquakes during that agricultural year (1959–1960) caused a postponement until 1965. The significant point here is that there does not exist a pool of experienced interviewers for this type of work. Since over 268,000 individuals were interviewed in a period of two months, there is probably a large margin of error in the data collected. It is reasonable to assume that for large groups of individuals within the total, errors in both directions cancel one another. However, for smaller groups this assumption may be less plausible. This pessimism seems especially in order for production data (in contrast to land-use information) which in many cases is based on memory. Since the farms to be used in the comparisons made here are all very large, there is some room for hope that written records were used in the answering of the questionnaires. Since the interviews were made immediately at the end of the agricultural year, the data collected is probably as accurate as any that might have been collected in any other way.

Although Chile has strict laws regulating the accessibility of individual farm data, it is not inconceivable that some farmers feared use of the data by CORA and thus distorted the facts. The census was taken just a few months after the Frei government was elected on an agrarian reform platform. However, since Chilean tradition is quite respectful of law, there is reason to hope that farmers did not fear use of the data in this manner, and thus the distortions from this source may not be too great.

Since data could not be obtained from the census on a per farm basis, a more exacting comparison, such as analysis of variance tests, could not be made. It is only possible to compare group averages and try to evaluate their implications. Personnel in the Census Bureau were given the list of *asentamientos* in the sample studied here, together with sufficient identification to locate the completed questionnaires for the particular farms involved. These same personnel then organized the data in the following manner: the sample farms were grouped as one; all other farms in the universe from which the sample was selected were grouped into provinces. In addition, data was obtained on a random sample of farms expropriated under the Agrarian Reform Law of July 1967. These were also grouped into provinces. The data of all the farms in the universe, or all farms which had been *asentamientos* for at least one agricultural year by August 1967, were obtained as a method of evaluating the representativeness of the sample. The selection of farms expropriated under the new law was made in order to compare the types of farms expropriated under the two laws. This comparison is necessary in order to determine whether or not projections based on the *asentamientos* which were expropriated under the old law will be valid for future *asentamientos*. The Census Bureau made available totals for each of the above groups, giving all the information obtained in the original census questionnaire.

The most serious problem in the use of the census data lies in the units for which the original data was collected, and the lack of complete identity with the units which are now *asentamientos*. Census data were collected on a per operations basis and not on a per farm basis. On the other hand, the *asentamientos* were formed from a legal farm unit. Thus it happened that an individual owner who operated two separate farms, even in widely different geographical areas, may have reported them to the census as one unit. Or a farmer may have rented parts of two or more farms and have reported them as one unit. There is no way in the questionnaire to separate out the information for one legal unit when such reporting was made.

There are further problems with the census data. Some farms on the list could not be located at all by the Census Bureau. In addition, some farms were operated partially by share croppers, each of whom reported separately. It was not always possible to locate all the reports from the former share croppers. The garden plots of *inquilinos* were reported separately, but the number and smallness of the units involved led to the elimination of these plots from consideration both in the census data collected and in the *asentamientos*. Since in most cases these plots were the same both in size and in quality before and after the expropriation, and since their production estimates would be subject to a high margin of error, it seemed not worth the high marginal cost to obtain this information from the census.

## Comparison of Asentamientos Before and After Expropriation

The first sets of data to be compared, then, will be the census data on the sample *asentamientos* and the CORA data on these same farms for the year 1966–1967. It will be remembered that the census data is for the year 1964–1965. Any comparison of productivity must recognize the high variability in year-to-year comparisons of farm output data due to weather factors. However, in Chile this factor is normally not of such serious proportions since almost all farm output in the area under consideration is either on irrigated land or produced by dryland methods, and thus is not sensitive to yearly variations in rainfall—except in years of very severe shortage such as 1968–1969. Of the eighteen farms in the sample, four were expropriated before the census was taken, and thus there is no prereform data from this source. One other could not be located and a sixth would have been compiled at such a prohibitive cost due to the large number of individuals (200) who were share croppers on the farm that it was eliminated.

This leaves for comparison twelve farms which are grouped in the data obtained from the census. Of these twelve, one was reported with another farm not in the sample as one unit. Another farm, though reported as a single unit, was only partially used to form one of the *asentamientos* in the sample. Fortunately, it was possible to use CORA prereform data on land use in these two cases to eliminate the extraneous information from the group totals. However, this correction applies only to land use and not to production. A third farm, though reported in the census in the same form as in the sample of *asentamientos,* had not released the accounts for the year 1966–1967 at the time this study was completed. This farm also had to be eliminated in the following comparisons. These adjustments leave only a very small number of farms in the final comparative analysis. We will use larger, though not completely identical groups in some of the following comparisons as a check on the validity of the comparisons made with the smaller group.

There are two ways that a farm may change its production: cultivate more of the land available, or use methods to improve the productivity per hectare of the land now in use. Although, obviously, production requires the use of inputs other than land, there is evidence that most *asentamientos* had no lack of labor or capital, so that either type of expansion should not have been difficult. We will look at both aspects to try to determine whether or not changes have been made in the farms now *asentamientos.*

With regard to the data, it is first pointed out that the amount of total land being considered is not precisely the same. The total area given for the eleven farms in the census data is 71,552 hectares, while that given in the CORA data on *asentamientos* is 70,532. Part of this discrepancy is due to the fact that land boundaries are not always precisely known and that, especially for the census figures, the amount of land in mountains and hills is often estimated. CORA officials now have the use of air-photographs which are presumably more accurate.

In order to interpret the data given in this and succeeding sections, the following manipulations with the census data must be kept in mind. For land-use data, we were fortunate in that the areas for total land, land in permanent crops, annual crops, and artificial and natural pasture for those farms for which we do not have *asentamiento* data, could be deleted from the census data. These same deletions could not be made for areas in specific crops nor for production of specific crops since CORA did not have this information on these particular farms. Thus, in the comparisons made on the use of land, we have precisely the same farms, but in the comparisons made on output per hectare, the farms are not the same. The census data include three rather sizable areas which the *asentamiento* data do not include. Since these three areas were operated by the same management and are contiguous to three of the farms in the *asentamiento* data, we make the assumption that the comparisons of output per hectare for particular crops are not changed significantly by the inclusion of these areas. The only reason to suppose that this is a bad assumption, given the same management and location, is the possibility that some sort of microclimatic difference or soil difference exists in spite of the proximity. From other information we have about the areas involved, we have no reason to suspect such differences.

Before showing the actual figures, we will describe a particular set of farms which must be considered separately. About 300 miles north of Santiago lies the rich valley of Choapa. This valley was originally one large farm that included 8,000 or more hectares of irrigated land contiguous with about 145,000 hectares of dry lands, hills, and mountains. At the beginning of Frei's administration this farm was held by the National Health Service and was sold to CORA as the first agrarian reform lands of the new administration. Thus, during the first year of the *asentamiento* experiment, this valley contained well over half of the 2,069 families formed into *asentamientos* and about half the total land as well as half the irrigated land. The valley had been divided into several administrative units by the Health Service. This division was maintained in the *asentamientos*. Two of the largest of these are in the sample studied by ICIRA. Since these two *asentamientos* are disproportionately large and also unrepresentative in ways to be explained, we make the comparisons of land use both with and without including them. Only one of these, which we shall call #1, was included in the census data for the period prior to expropriation.

The farms in the Choapa valley are unrepresentative of the present and future *asentamientos* for several reasons. They are extremely isolated geographically both from other CORA activities and from any other center of urban or rural activity. Previously most of the land was farmed by some sharecropping scheme; some individuals had up to ten hectares in "garden plots." CORA has changed these arrangements very little. Thus in both the Choapa farms in the sample only about half the members actually contribute any work outside their own garden plots. There is no other area similar in size, isolation, and organization which CORA has bought or expropriated since the purchase of Choapa. The validity of using such a sample is based on the assumption that it represents not only the current situation, but also the characteristics of future *asentamientos*. Since it appears highly unlikely that Choapa is similar to any future area, we make special note of it in the following discussions.

The columns of Table 5–1 indicate the percentage of land use in various categories. The confusing part of these figures is the large discrepancy found in the last two columns between census data and CORA data. The last column is composed mostly of land in hills, mountains, forests, and infrastructure. Now it is difficult to imagine how this category could have been changed by the reform. However, if we take the last two columns together, there is much more consistency. The only interpretation of this apparent inconsistency is that farm managers or owners in answering the census questionnaire had a different definition for some lands than did CORA officials. These lands are probably marginal as to whether they should be classified as hills or as natural pasture, when, in fact, they were used for pasture.

The first two rows in Table 5–1 represent identical farms for two different periods. Tests of significance are made difficult in that census data are available only as a single total for the eleven farms. If, however, we make the reasonable assumption that the variance within this group is the same as the variance within the same farm group for 1966–1967, then we can test for the significance of the differences of the means of the two groups. Based on this assumption, a *t* test was used to test the significance of the differences in the average amount of land used by the eleven farms prior to and after expropriation for each of the categories of Table 5–1. As can be seen from Table 5–2, there is no significant difference in the means for any of the categories of land use with the exception of land in natural pasture. Since there is no difference in other uses of land, and since both sets represent the same farms, this difference in natural pasture can only be attributed, as indicated above, to some confusion in the precise distinction between natural pasture and hilly land used for pasture.

If the results of Table 5–2 are representative of the entire universe of *asentamientos* in 1966–1967, the implication is that there was no change significantly different from zero in the use of land on these farms as compared with the year 1964–1965, when they were still under the control of

**Table 5-1**

**Land Use on Farms Before Expropriation and as Asentamientos**

| Sample | Hectares of Total Land | Percent of Land in Permanent Crops | Percent of Land in Annual Crops | Percent of Land in Artificial Pasture | Percent of Land Fallow | Percent of Land in Natural Pasture | Percent of Land in Other Uses |
|---|---|---|---|---|---|---|---|
| Census data 1964–1965 for 11 Farms | 71,552 | .2 | 3.5 | 0.9 | 6.0 | 28 | 61.4 |
| CORA data 1966–1967 for 11 *Asentamientos* | 70,337 | .1 | 3.6 | 1.0 | 0.4 | 14 | 80.9 |
| CORA data 1966–1967 for 17 *Asentamientos* (the entire sample) | 146,808 | .2 | 2.4 | 0.5 | 0.3 | 57.2 | 40 |
| CORA data 1966–1967 (the sample with *Asentamiento* #1 eliminated) | 72,501 | .4 | 4.5 | 1.0 | 0.6 | 13.3 | 80 |
| CORA data 1966–1967 (with Choapa eliminated) | 36,631 | .9 | 7.5 | 2.0 | 1.1 | 23.1 | 65 |
| Census data 1964–1965 (for the entire set of farms in the universe) [a] | 160,602 | .2 | 4.3 | 0.9 | 4.9 | 29.8 | 59 |

[a] Only thirty-two of the universe of fifty-three farms were located in the Census Bureau.

**Table 5-2**

**Mean Number of Hectares of Land in Various Uses for Group of Eleven Farms (1964-1965 and 1966-1967)**

| Use of Land | Census Data 1964-1965 | Cora Data 1966-1967 | t-Test for Differences of Means |
|---|---|---|---|
| Land in permanent crops | 16.0 | 10.2 | Not Significant |
| Land in annual crops | 225.0 | 230.9 | Not Significant |
| Land in artificial pasture | 59.1 | 63.6 | Not Significant |
| Land fallow | 28.5 | 28.3 | Not Significant |
| Land in natural pasture | 809.2 | 1840.6 | Significant at 1% |

the former owners. Before this conclusion was accepted, a test was made to determine whether there is a significant difference between the eleven *asentamientos* used above and the seventeen in the original sample. Table 5-3 shows the means of the amount of land used in the various categories for the seventeen *asentamientos* and the subset of eleven. As indicated in the last column, there is no evidence of significant difference.

Table 5-4 shows the means in land-use categories for the entire set of

**Table 5-3**

**Mean Number of Hectares in Land-Use Categories for Subset of Eleven Asentamientos and the Sample of Seventeen**

| Land Use | Eleven Asentamientos [a] | Seventeen Asentamientos [b] | Significance |
|---|---|---|---|
| Permanent crops | 10.2 | 19.5 | None |
| Annual crops | 230.9 | 211.1 | None |
| Artificial pasture | 63.6 | 46.0 | None |
| Total | 304.6 | 276.6 | None |

[a] 27% of the total land used.
[b] 33% of the total land used.

**Table 5-4**

**Average Number of Hectares in Land Use Categories for Subset of Eleven Farms and Thirty-two Farms from Census Data**

| Land Use | Eleven Farms | Thirty-two Farms |
|---|---|---|
| Permanent crops | 16.0 | 17.2 |
| Annual crops | 225.0 | 199.7 |
| Artificial pasture | 59.1 | 62.9 |
| Total | 300.1 | 279.8 |

data from the census for thirty-two farms, and the subset of eleven used in the test above. Although there is no way to test the significance of these differences, the knowledge that the variance is high in both groups leads us to the conclusion that the differences in means is not significant.

It is further desirable to know the reliability of the random sample of the seventeen *asentamientos*. (It should be recalled here that there were fifty-three *asentamientos* in the entire universe, and that the original sample drawn contained twenty *asentamientos,* three having been eliminated for reasons already explained.) Table 5–5 shows the means and standard er-

**Table 5–5**

**Mean and Standard Errors for Number of Hectares in Land Use Categories for Seventeen Asentamientos of the Sample**

| Land Use | Mean | Standard Error | t Statistic [b] |
|---|---|---|---|
| Permanent crops [a] | 19.9 | 8.8 | 2.21 |
| Annual crops [a] | 211.1 | 40.8 | 5.1 |
| Artificial pasture [a] | 46.0 | 14.8 | 3.1 |
| Fallow [a] | 23.5 | 12.3 | 1.9 |
| Total for crops (including artificial pasture) | 276.6 | 43.8 | 6.2 |
| Percent of total land in crops | 32.9 | 7.5 | 4.3 |

[a] Hectares.
[b] A *t* value greater than two implies that at the 95% level of confidence the sample mean does not differ significantly from the universe mean.

rors of the amount of land in the various categories for the seventeen *asentamientos*. These results support the hypothesis that land use on the *asentamientos* of the universe is not significantly different from land use on those in this sample.

These tests support the interpretation that there was no change in land use after expropriation on those *asentamientos* in existence in 1967.

## Comparison of One- and Two-Year-Old Asentamientos

It might be argued that it is too soon to expect changes. Some of the *asentamientos* in this sample had existed as such for only one year. One answer to this argument is that prior to expropriation there were studies made outlining plans for the efficient use of the land. Further, there was virtually no constraint on credit for seeds and fertilizer. If it is true, as the proponents of agrarian reform have argued, that there is an excess of farm labor and that the land currently in natural pasture could easily be put to use, then it is not too much to expect that an immediate change might occur. One way to test whether or not time makes a difference is to test whether a change in land use occurs between the first and the second year of the *asentamiento*. That is, if it is too much to expect a change after only one year as an *asentamiento,* we might expect some change after two years. There are two ways to test such a hypothesis: comparison of the same *asentamientos* over a two-year period and a cross-section comparison of *asentamientos* with one and two years' experience. Since ICIRA did a preliminary study of *asentamientos* for the 1965–1966 agricultural year, there is data available on five *asentamientos* for a two-year period. Within the sample of seventeen, there are eight *asentamientos* with two years' experience and nine with one year's experience. In neither the two-year comparison for the same *asentamiento* nor the cross-section comparison is there indication of significant difference in the use of land. The cross-section test was also made on a subset of these figures by eliminating Choapa in the two-year-old *asentamientos* and one extreme case from the set of one-year-olds. Since these farms had such large amounts of mountainous, unusable land, the percentages of land use are distorted. Comparing these two subsets of one-year-old with two-year-old *asentamientos* also leads to the conclusion of no significant difference in land use. Tables 5–6, 5–7, and 5–8 present the results of these tests.

**Table 5–6**

**Land Use on One- and Two-Year-Old Asentamientos**

| Land Use | Five Asentamientos 1965–1966 | Five Asentamientos 1966–1967 | Significance |
|---|---|---|---|
| Permanent crops [a] | 41.9 | 42.1 | None |
| Annual crops [a] | 167.0 | 185.5 | None |
| Artificial pasture [a] | 74.1 | 71.2 | None |
| Percent of total land in use | 28 | 31 | None |
| Percent of cultivatable land in use | 74.3 | 74.8 | None |

[a] In mean hectares.

## Application of Results to Future Asentamientos

Finally, it is necessary to know whether these *asentamientos,* formed from farms expropriated under the 1962 law, can be expected to be representative of those formed from farms expropriated under the 1967 law. Using census data on farms grouped according to zone, a cross-section comparison was made between samples expropriated under each of the

**Table 5–7**

**Land Use on One- and Two-Year-Old Asentamientos for the Same Agricultural Year**

| Land Use | One-Year-Old *Asentamientos* | Two-Year-Old *Asentamientos* | Significance |
|---|---|---|---|
| Land in crops [a] | 249.5 | 307.1 | None |
| Percent of cultivatable land in use | 74.2 | 70.8 | None |
| Percent of total land in use | 35.6 | 30.0 | None |

[a] In mean hectares.

**Table 5–8**

**Land Use on One- and Two-Year-Old Asentamientos for the Same Agricultural Year with Extreme Cases Eliminated**

| Land Use | One-Year-Old *Asentamientos* | Two-Year-Old *Asentamientos* | Significance |
|---|---|---|---|
| Permanent crops [a] | 5.2 | 43.5 | None |
| Annual crops [a] | 219.7 | 147.1 | None |
| Artificial pasture [a] | 39.6 | 65.5 | None |
| Total land cultivated [a] | 264.5 | 256.1 | None |
| Percent of cultivated land in use | 71.0 | 75.6 | None |
| Percent of total land land in use | 39.9 | 39.5 | None |

[a] In mean hectares.

two laws. The sample of farms expropriated after July 1967, was drawn from the universe of farms expropriated between that date and February 1968. These farms would, for the most part, constitute the additional *asentamientos* for the agricultural year 1968–1969. The results of these tests, comparing these farms with those farms already *asentamientos* in 1967, are shown in Table 5–9.

It can be seen that there are significant differences in the amount of land in artificial pasture and in the percentage of cultivatable land in crops. Also the amount of land in natural pasture is significantly less on farms now being expropriated than on previously expropriated farms.[a] This implies that

[a] It is assumed that the definitional problem for natural pasture mentioned above does not exist in this case. The reason for the assumption is that *this* comparison uses all census data and the previous one compared census data with that collected by ICIRA in two different years by a different set of investigators.

**Table 5–9**

**Test of Differences in Land Use of Farms Expropriated under the 1962 Law and of Farms Expropriated Under the 1967 Law**

| Land Use | New Law Expropriations | Old Law Expropriations | Significance |
|---|---|---|---|
| Annual crops [a] | 15.3 | 10.2 | None |
| Permanent crops [a] | 276.3 | 194.6 | None |
| Artificial pasture [a] | 274.5 | 65.1 | Significant at 95% level |
| Natural pasture [a] | 766.9 | 1089.5 | Significant at 95% level |
| Percent of cropland fertilizer | 49.4 | 47.7 | None |
| Percent of cultivatable land in crops | 60.7 | 23.9 | Significant at 95% level |

[a] In mean hectares.

there is not as much land available for expansion on the farms that will become *asentamientos* in 1968. The main concern here is whether or not these latter farms are less well managed than the already expropriated farms because of the change in the criteria for expropriation allowed by the law. One test of good management has been the amount of land in natural pasture. The test here shows that farms more recently expropriated were in this sense better managed prior to expropriation than were farms expropriated earlier.

A second criterion of good management might be the amount of fertilizer used. Since the census questionnaire did not ask for the amount of fertilizer used, but rather the amount of land on which it was used, we compare the percentage of land in use with the percentage of land fertilized. The test leads to the conclusion that there is no significant difference between the two sets of farms in the amount of land fertilized.

What, in summary, are the conclusions to be drawn from the above tests? (1) The evidence now available is insufficient to support the hypothesis that the *asentamiento* structure either increases or lessens the intensity of land use over the previous structure of private ownership. This conclusion continues to hold after two years of the *asentamiento* structure. (2) For the farms expropriated prior to July 1967, even though some improvement in land use does take place after more experience as *asentamientos,* there is reason to believe that there is more possibility of improvement in the use of land than for farms expropriated after July 1967. The evidence shows significantly less land in natural pasture on farms expropriated under the later law as opposed to earlier expropriations.

## Output per Hectare of Different Crops

Another possible means of increasing production is to change the output per hectare on the land actually in use. Again, we might ask why changes in productivity would be expected. It has been claimed that large land-owners were for the most part bad managers. If the claim is true, it could be expected that no attempt was made to use the best seeds, the most modern methods of planting, or the most productive type and amount of fertilizer. In the case of the *asentamientos,* all purchases of inputs were

**Table 5–10**

**Ratios of Productivities on Farms and Asentamientos to Productivities for the Entire Geographic Area and Ratios Weighted by Percentage of Land in Crop**

| Crop | Ratio for 11 Sample Farms from Census Data 1964–1965 | Ratio Weighted | Ratio for 11 Sample *Asentamientos* 1966–1967 | Ratio Weighted | Ratio for 17 *Asentamientos* 1966–1967 | Ratio Weighted | Ratio for 32 Farms from Census Data 1964–1965 | Ratio Weighted |
|---|---|---|---|---|---|---|---|---|
|  | (1) | (2) | (3) | (4) | (5) | (6) | (7) | (8) |
| Sugar Beets | 1.47 | 0.029 | 1.23 | 0.025 | 0.90 | 0.036 | 1.47 | 0.014 |
| Wheat | 1.35 | 0.648 | 1.30 | 0.410 | 1.20 | 0.373 | 1.39 | 0.724 |
| Barley | 0.76 | 0.114 | 1.42 | 0.185 | 1.24 | 0.180 | 0.74 | 0.073 |
| Oats | 1.39 | 0.014 | — | — | 1.32 | 0.013 | 1.39 | 0.008 |
| Rice | 0.32 | 0.009 | 2.36 | 0.113 | 2.30 | 0.085 | 0.76 | 0.021 |
| Corn | 1.07 | 0.107 | 1.24 | 0.179 | 1.10 | 0.152 | 1.18 | 0.116 |
| Beans | 1.48 | 0.148 | 1.37 | 0.274 | 1.33 | 0.271 | 1.32 | 0.095 |
| Green Peas | 0.16 | — | 3.75 | 0.038 | 3.75 | 0.030 | 0.47 | 0.001 |
| Chick Peas | — | — | 1.98 | 0.040 | 1.98 | 0.032 | 0.27 | 0.001 |
| Potatoes | 1.19 | 0.051 | 1.05 | 0.063 | 1.10 | 0.055 | 1.08 | 0.075 |
| Sun Flower | 1.57 | 0.094 | 1.21 | 0.065 | 1.23 | 0.049 | 1.50 | 0.042 |
| Tobacco | 0.80 | 0.001 | 1.08 | 0.001 | 1.08 | 0.054 | 0.80 | 0.001 |
| Total |  | 1.215 |  | 1.393 |  | 1.330 |  | 1.171 |

made through CORA, and each *asentamiento* had a technical expert always available to it without cost. Therefore, it is not unreasonable to expect some improvement in output per hectare of the various crops. It is impossible to make comparisons except for production of specific annual crops. Census data on the output for some crops such as melons, tomatoes, and fruits are not available. Column 1 of Table 5–10 shows the ratio of output per hectare on the eleven farms prior to expropriation to the average output per hectare in all provinces from which the sample of eleven farms is drawn. Column 3 shows this ratio for these same eleven farms as *asentamientos.* (In both cases the denominator is for 1964–1965.) Column

5 shows this ratio for all seventeen *asentamientos* in the sample, while column 7 shows the prereform ratios for all those farms expropriated by 1967 for which census data can be located. Columns 5 and 7 are given as some check on the representativeness of the sample of eleven farms. By examining specific crop ratios, we can see that the results are mixed. Some productivities are increased, others decreased on the *asentamientos*. To form a composite, each ratio was weighted by the percentage of land in the particular crop. This percentage is related to the total amount of land in all those crops for which the figures on output are available. These figures are then added for the crops in order to give an overall index of productivity for the two groups of farms. Table 5–10 shows the calculations for the eleven farms from the census data for 1964–1965 and the same eleven farms, two years later as *asentamientos*. These same calculations are made for the entire sample of seventeen *asentamientos* for 1966–1967 and the entire set of thirty-two farms for 1964–1965.

From the calculations made, it can be seen that there is a larger overall productivity index in the *asentamientos*. It is possible that this result indicates an improvement. We must ask, however, to what degree the improvement is greater than that which would have been the case on these same farms in 1966–1967 had the former owners continued in control. The main crops to have significantly improved are barley, rice, corn, and green peas. In the cases of barley and green peas, agricultural data indicate large increases in productivity for the country as a whole between 1964–1965 and 1966–1967.[1] (Had data by province in 1966–1967 been available, the *country* changes in productivity could have been incorporated by using these data in the denominator for the productivity ratios.) Since *asentamientos* were too few in number to have affected the country-wide productivities, the national increases cannot be due to their influence. Therefore it is possible that productivity in these crops would have gone up on these farms in any case. On the other hand, the overall productivity for corn declined in this period. The very large productivity figure for rice is the result of an unusually high output on one *asentamiento*. However, this particular farm had such high costs of operation that "profits" were highly negative. The contribution of this output is, therefore, of dubious advantage.

We are left with the conclusion that it is possible, but not at all certain that the *asentamiento* organization has led to some increase in overall productivity on the farms involved.

**Macroeconomic Impact of Asentamiento Production**

The fundamental interest of this paper is whether or not the agrarian reform is capable of having an impact on the whole of agriculture in the macroeconomic sense. So far we have considered only the microeconomic impact on the individual farms. Two conditions are necessary in order that improvements at the farm level be felt throughout agriculture. The farms involved must constitute a significant portion of the total agricultural land. Second, improvements on these farms must not be offset by opposite effects on farms not expropriated. Alternatively, the farms involved in the reform areas may be a smaller portion of the total, if the nonexpropriated farms, through fear of expropriation, actually improve significantly. In this second case, the agrarian reform would indirectly have caused an improvement in the overall production of the agricultural sector. This latter case is not usually the one presented in arguments favoring agrarian reform, but it may not be unimportant in a country such as Chile.

The first question to be tackled here will be whether or not the area in agrarian reform farms will be a significant portion of total agricultural area. Between January 1965 and December 1967, some 778 thousand hectares of land were formed into *asentamientos* supporting 8,252 families. Of this total area, 84,611 hectares were irrigated. This makes an average of approximately 94 hectares per family, with an average of 10.2 hectares of irrigated land. According to the Institute for Research on Natural Resources (IREN), there existed approximately 24.5 million hectares of land on farms in 1967 between the northern border and the island areas of southern Chile. Of this amount, 1.6 million hectares were irrigated and 4.8 million were without agricultural usefulness. The amount of land in *asentamientos* in 1967 was too small to have an impact on all of agriculture. However, the number of families which has been set up as a goal of the agrarian reform program is 100,000. If each of the *asentamientos* continued to average about 94 hectares per family, then the goal of 100,000 families would imply that about 38 percent of all agricultural land would be *asentamientos*. The situation is even more striking if we consider only the irrigated land. If each *asentamiento* continues to include on the average 10 hectares of irrigated land per *asentado,* and if the amount of irrigated land in Chile does not expand, the *asentamientos* would control about 63 percent of such land. It is unrealistic to suppose that 63 percent of the land presently irrigated would ever be expropriated. Expropriations can affect only the area in excess of 80 basic hectares of large farms.

It is also probably unrealistic to suppose that the goal of 100,000 families will be reached. On the other hand, it is not unreasonable that before January 1971 when a new president will take office, between 30,000 and 40,000 families will have been constituted into *asentamientos*. (These projections were made in 1968. As of December 31, 1969, slightly less than 17,000 families were established in *asentamientos*.) It is also quite possible that the number of irrigated hectares per *asentado* will be reduced. This reduction will take place through the adding of members to *asentamientos* already in existence. One estimate which has been used, but not in print, is that the goal of seven irrigated hectares per *asentado* family should be sought. If we take the number of families to be 40,000 before January

1971, and assume that each will control about 7 hectares of irrigated land, the amount in *asentamientos* will be about 17 percent. On the reasonable assumption that more land will be brought under irrigation before 1971, the percentage would be less. Conceivably, then, an output change of, say 20 percent on *asentamientos* could effect a 2 or 3 percent change in total agricultural output. Actually, however, the amount of land held by *asentamientos* as of December 31, 1969 reduces the affect possible by 1970 to about 1 percent.

This is not the place to estimate the probabilities that expropriations will or will not be stopped after January 1971. It is simply stated here that even if they are stopped, the amount of land held in *asentamientos* relative to the total amount of agricultural land will not be insignificant by 1971.

## Possible Indirect Impact of the Agrarian Reform

We now examine the indirect impact on total agricultural production. There are two ways to investigate whether or not any change in output or in agricultural investment could be attributed to a reaction to the agrarian reform law. The more correct way would be to work out a model to explain agricultural output and agricultural investment, then to see whether departures from the estimates provided by the model can be attributed to agrarian reform laws. In other words, a systematic departure after 1964, or even after 1962, could be attributed to a reaction to the law. Such an analysis would require a separate study which, unfortunately, has not been made. As a rather less sophisticated way to get at this problem, without trying to explain output or investment, a trend in agricultural production as well as in various types of investment was estimated. We can then see whether or not departures from the trends are consistent with a reaction to the agrarian reform law.

It is rational for private owners to have either a positive or a negative reaction to the law, depending on their subjective evaluation of both their situation as landowners and the extent to which the government will carry out its intentions. Production in the short run could be less than the predicted trend if owners, believing the future to be uncertain, simply lose interest. It might also be less if investment in machinery declined. There is slightly more reason to suppose output on other farms would have increased in the short run between 1962 and 1967 when the only justification for expropriation was bad management. Farm owners who thought that they could lessen chances of their land being expropriated by planting some of their pasture land in crops could have created a spurt in output during that period. Positive and negative responses could have balanced out so that no reaction is observable.

Table 5–11 shows the actual and predicted trend values for the index

**Table 5–11**

**Actual and Fitted Values for Index of
Agricultural Production (1939 $=$ 100)**

| Year | Actual Values | Fitted Values |
|------|---------------|---------------|
| 1939 | 100.0 | 92.41 |
| 1940 | 97.9 | 95.01 |
| 1941 | 97.9 | 97.61 |
| 1942 | 101.6 | 100.2 |
| 1943 | 106.8 | 102.8 |
| 1944 | 113.1 | 105.4 |
| 1945 | 109.2 | 108.0 |
| 1946 | 113.8 | 110.6 |
| 1947 | 110.9 | 113.2 |
| 1948 | 114.6 | 115.8 |
| 1949 | 115.6 | 118.4 |
| 1950 | 114.3 | 121.0 |
| 1951 | 117.3 | 123.6 |
| 1952 | 115.3 | 126.2 |
| 1953 | 122.3 | 128.8 |
| 1954 | 128.1 | 131.4 |
| 1955 | 131.9 | 134.0 |
| 1956 | 134.3 | 136.6 |
| 1957 | 134.1 | 139.2 |
| 1958 | 144.4 | 141.8 |
| 1959 | 140.5 | 144.4 |
| 1960 | 147.0 | 147.0 |
| 1961 | 153.4 | 149.6 |
| 1962 | 152.7 | 152.2 |
| 1963 | 152.4 | 154.8 |
| 1964 | 163.1 | 157.4 |
| 1965 | 159.8 | 160.0 |
| 1966 | 168.7 | 162.6 |
| 1967 | 173.9 | 165.2 |

Note: $In = 89.8 + 2.6t$     $\bar{R}^2 = 0.95$
        (1.9) (0.11)
where   $In =$ index   of   production   and
          $t =$ year.
Source: Actual values from Table 2–1.

of agricultural production from 1939 to 1967. The output for any calendar year always implies that most of the planting was done the previous calendar year. The first reform law was passed in 1962, so the 1963 index would be the relevant one. The second law was not passed until 1967, but the election of 1964 was conducted on a platform of carrying out an effective reform. One could interpret the above trend indexes for 1966 and 1967 as positive reactions to the reform.

There is more reason to believe that a decline in agricultural investment might result from fear of expropriation. Such a decline could affect production even in the short run if, for example, it involved a decline in the rate of investment in machinery resulting from the owners' fear of capital loss if their farms were expropriated. Even a slight fear of expropriation would be expected to cause a decline in the area of investment for permanent improvements in the land itself. In part, this problem could be avoided by a well-written law. Professor Rodan (in private conversation) has argued that uncertainty and unnecessary fear would be eliminated if all farms definitely to be expropriated were announced immediately. Also, a law that, regardless of the payment for the land itself, assured payment in full

**Table 5–12**

**Actual and Fitted Values for Total Investment in Agriculture and Investment in Agricultural Machinery (millions of E° of 1965)**

| Year | Total Agriculture [a] | | Machinery [b] | |
|------|---------------|---------------|---------------|---------------|
|      | Actual Values | Fitted Values | Actual Values | Fitted Values |
| 1956 | 301.5 | 275.1 | 59.50 | 52.93 |
| 1957 | 278.8 | 286.8 | 70.10 | 55.48 |
| 1958 | 305.8 | 298.5 | 40.60 | 58.03 |
| 1959 | 235.9 | 310.3 | 33.40 | 60.58 |
| 1960 | 328.4 | 322.0 | 61.50 | 63.13 |
| 1961 | 392.3 | 333.7 | 87.50 | 65.69 |
| 1962 | 327.4 | 345.4 | 71.80 | 68.24 |
| 1963 | 360.6 | 357.1 | 80.50 | 70.79 |
| 1964 | 371.4 | 368.8 | 73.20 | 73.34 |
| 1965 | 376.1 | 380.5 | 66.00 | 75.89 |

[a] $I = 64.4 + 11.7t$ $\quad \bar{R}^2 = 0.53$
$\quad$ (89.1) $\quad$ (3.9)
where $I$ = total investment and $t$ = year.
[b] $I = 7.0 + 2.6t$ $\quad \bar{R}^2 = 0.21$
$\quad$ (39.3) $\quad$ (1.7)
where $I$ = investment in machinery and $t$ = year.
Source: Actual values from ODEPLAN, mimeographed.

for all equipment and improvements made after the law was passed could forestall any possible decline in this area.

Trend values for total investment and investment in machinery from 1956 to 1965 were estimated from unpublished data of ODEPLAN on agricultural investment. These estimates are given in Table 5–12. In neither case is the fit good. In both cases the 1965 level of investment is slightly below the trend value. Without a pattern from 1962, we can make no implications from these results. In the case of other types of investment, there is no trend and it is, therefore, impossible to make any statements about what investment might have been. Investment in livestock has increased considerably since 1962, but special government incentives of a very complex nature make it extremely difficult to judge the meaning of this increase. Investment in artificial pasture fluctuated within a very narrow range between 1956 and 1965. But the average between 1964 and 1967 is clearly higher than the average for the eight previous years.

The examination of investment behavior, therefore, does not clearly support an interpretation of lower investment through fear of expropriation. A complete study on agricultural investment would be required to state more conclusively whether or not the interpretation is supported.

In summary, with regard to the impact of the reform on the rest of agriculture, it can be stated that output data are consistent with, but do not conclusively support, an interpretation that an increase in output could have resulted from a desire to forestall expropriation. The impact on agricultural investment is not clear: the data do not unambiguously support any interpretation relating investment to fear of expropriation. It may be that landowners did not really begin to fear expropriation until after July 1967, when it became possible to expropriate land for the motive of size alone. In this case, it is not yet possible to evaluate reactions.

### The Future of Asentamiento Production

Thus far in interpreting the future of *asentamiento* production, it has been assumed that whatever changes or lack thereof which have occurred on the *asentamiento* from the previous status will maintain themselves beyond the present organizational structure into the period of titled ownership. It is useful to examine alternative reactions of the post-*asentamiento*. There are three different models which could suggest the direction that might be taken by the *asentamientos* in a later period. The small propietor has always existed in Chile. We might suppose that *asentamientos* will be parceled and that the owners of the parceled land would operate the land as owners of small plots of land do at present. Or we might expect owners of the new parcels to behave as do the present owners of land parceled by CORA before the *asentamiento* experiment began. Finally, it is possible that the future organization of the farms may be more like the present *asentamientos*. We may gain some insight into future *asentamiento* possibilities by examining each of these models.

It is recalled that a previous experiment in gradual turnover of land was conducted with some Church property under the direction of INPROA, a privately supported organization that has the same function as CORA in its relation to the farm. For the four farms involved in this experiment—two after two years' experience and two after three years—INPROA reports striking results: the amount of land in natural pasture went from 18.9 to 0 percent; output per hectares increased on nearly all crops; and the value of output nearly doubled.[2] There is, however, reason to doubt the reported size of this improvement, since it is highly doubtful that INPROA was able to obtain data on prereform land use of the farms.[3] It is possible that former resident laborers remembered the data on land in natural pasture, but it is difficult to believe that their memory of how much wheat, beans, or other specific crops were produced would be very accurate. The INPROA organization was similar to that of the CORA *asentamientos*. The INPROA improvement was made within a two-year period. It is clear that if the CORA experiment would begin to perform as well as that of INPROA there would be large improvements from the present situation even if the structure of the organization remained the same.

Data on land use for different sized farms in Chile indicate that family-size farms have as large a percentage of land in natural pasture as do larger farms.[4] According to the 1965 census data, although there is a systematic inverse relation between size of farms and percent of land in natural pastures, the relation does not hold when the farms are ranked according to the number of irrigated hectares. (The 1964 data do not allow comparisons of the amount of irrigated land itself in natural pasture, but farms were ranked according to the number of irrigated hectares, and the percentage in natural pasture applies to the total land.)

If it is true that credit is more available to large farms than to small farms, then no conclusion can be drawn from actual land use. Credit may be a constraint for family-size landowners. The evidence cited in Chapter 2 showed that actual credit was distributed to large landholders in greater proportion than their holdings. This in itself does not prove that credit was less available to smaller landowners. It is possible that they did not ask for credit.

There is one other way the evidence on land use by large and small landowners may be interpreted. Use of artificial pasture to increase the number of animals that can be grazed per hectare may be a sophisticated technique which has not occurred to owners of family-size farms. Especially when animals are raised primarily for consumption, these owners may not be aware of possibilities for grazing other than the use of natural pasture.

Neither of the interpretations offered here can be demonstrated. We must, therefore, admit that there is no clear evidence that owners of family-size farms would use land more intensively if given the same access to credit and information on techniques available to the large landowners.

Farms parceled by CORA before the present *asentamientos* might present another possibility for the *asentamientos* if they are parceled. CORA gave titles to these earlier farms after providing each parcel with the infrastructure necessary for a self-sufficient unit. The *asentamiento* was intended to accomplish two goals: lower the cost by the use of available infrastructure through cooperative ownership, and train the peasant to be a farm manager. If the second goal is accomplished, the results of previous CORA parcelizations would presumably underestimate the potential of the new parcelizations. In 1964 Paul Aldunate studied these earlier CORA farms.[5] The study was conducted by the comparison of a random sample of these farms with a random sample of privately owned farms. The selection of private farms was limited to those specializing in annual crops rather than in fruits, vineyards, or livestock. The average size of the CORA farms was 22 hectares while the average size of the private farms was 214 hectares.

The results of the Aldunate study, although inconclusive, do not support a hypothesis of more intensive land use by small landowners. These results will be considered under two aspects: the percent of land cultivated and the output per hectare. The author does not distinguish between natural pasture and artificial pasture. However, family-size farms rarely make use of artificial pasture. It is probable that the figure for the land in pasture refers to natural pasture for the CORA farms. There is no way to make the same guess for the private farms. The percent of cultivatable land in pasture was given at 12 percent for the CORA farms and 15 percent for the private farms. This particular information does indicate that land is used more intensively on CORA farms than on the larger, privately owned farms, but only to a slight degree.

Gross output per hectare was reported to be higher on the larger farms. This result holds with respect both to total land and cultivatable land. Output per man is higher on the larger farms. Only when the labor cost on the CORA family farms is taken to be zero is net output per hectare higher on these farms. Even in this case, net output per man-day worked is lower on the family farms.

There is much to be criticized in the above study. There is no way of knowing to what degree the private farms in the sample were similar to the CORA farms prior to their expropriation, and this author has made no attempt to evaluate the issue. Furthermore, the number of nonrespondents for both CORA and private farms was very high, over 50 percent. Since the interviews were on a personal basis, "nonrespondent" meant direct refusal to participate in the interview. It is, therefore, possible that neither the CORA farms nor the private farms are representative.

What, then, can be expected from the *asentamientos* in the future? If the *asentamientos* are parceled, the evidence now available suggests that there will be little significant difference in their behavior after parcelization. Obviously, this statement is highly speculative and does not allow for the changes in attitude, in management ability, and in what Joan Robinson calls "animal spirit," that could result from the *asentamiento* training. Although some *asentamientos* have been very successful and from them CORA can learn what contributes to a successful *asentamiento* experience, the crucial importance of the training aspect of the *asentamiento* has been emphasized by our examination of family-sized farms and earlier parcelizations. Thus, if there is a serious concern for production, evidence does suggest that every effort must be made to make the *asentamiento* training experience effective.

The data on farms expropriated under the new agrarian reform law compared to farms expropriated under the earlier law show that there is less room for expansion on the newer *asentamientos*. It requires more sophistication to improve yields than to expand the amount of land used; therefore, it is even more necessary that the *asentamiento* training experience be effective if increased production is to be achieved.

**Impact of Income
Redistribution: Savings
and Demand Shifts**

The argument that a redistribution of income from landowners to workers will lead to increased demand for low-cost industrial products and, therefore, encourage investment in the industrial sector must be examined more closely.

From the point of view of demand itself, this argument has two implications: (1) that the current holders of land actually consume fewer domestic goods than would be consumed if income were distributed differently; and (2) that current holders of the land demand chiefly luxury products for which the potential for induced investment is not great, while the proposed new holders would demand goods which could be mass produced.

These implications of redistributing income require assumptions or evidence about the consumption behavior of both groups as well as evidence about the current and potential structure of the industries involved.

From the point of view of savings, an income redistribution that increases growth potential must affect either the amount of savings or the uses to which savings are put. Unless the marginal propensity of higher-income earners to save is greater than that of lower-income earners, total savings will not be decreased by the redistribution. The most important issue may be the *use* of savings. Long-run growth can be increased if the productivity of investment is increased. Investment in housing and foreign exchange is not as productive as investment in plant and equipment. What is needed to justify a case for redistribution of income on these grounds is not only evidence concerning the use of savings by current high-income holders, but also an assumption that savings will, in fact, be used differently by the potential receivers of this income. In order that savings be used more productively by the proposed new-income receivers, there is one further requirement: there must be either increased investment in agriculture itself or some mechanism by which the savings can be transferred to the industrial sector.

A further aspect of the use of savings must be raised here. It is possible that plant and equipment cannot be increased without imports. In this case a shift from consumption of imports to consumption of domestically produced goods and services through income redistribution may allow the expansion. However, even if this shift occurs, a full employment economy would not be able to increase domestic production and simultaneously keep exports constant. If exports decrease as much as imports decrease there is no improvement in the amount of foreign exchange available to buy capital goods. Therefore, at least in the short run, better use of savings would not be sufficient. Total savings must not decrease. In the case where imports are not the only source of capital equipment, a redistribution which decreases savings will in the short run create inflation in a full employment economy. (Full employment here refers to plant capacity, not to the labor force. If plant and equipment are already fully utilized, employment of more labor will not help.)

In this chapter we investigate the empirical evidence which will support or reject the hypothesis that the agrarian reform in Chile can, by effecting a redistribution of income in the agricultural sector, lead to an increased growth in the industrial sector.

In the expansion-of-market hypothesis three things are necessary in order that growth be increased by the redistribution. It is first required that the industrial structure be such that expanded markets will lead to the kind of modernization that decreases unit costs. Second, the redistribution of income which in fact results from the reform must be large enough to effect such a widening of markets. Finally, the expenditure behavior of those who receive the additional income must be significantly different from that of those who were the former recipients of the income.

In the use-of-savings hypothesis two requirements must be met: savings must in fact be used more productively, and there must be either excess capacity or no decrease in savings.

There is another way to interpret the hypothesis that income redistribution will be an improvement through the widening of markets for domestically produced goods. Installed plant and equipment may be underutilized. The high costs implied by this underutilization may be supported through high tariffs. In this case a redistribution, even with a decrease in savings could, in principle, increase the level of income without inflation. This increase in the level of income is a once-for-all change and does not imply a change in the long-run growth rate. But the presence of excess capacity with a simultaneous improvement in the use of savings would allow the long run growth rate to increase without inflation even if savings decreased. On the other hand, the failure to use savings more productively, together with a decrease in savings would imply a decline in long-run growth regardless of the higher current level of income.

We will investigate the savings and consumption behavior of the two classes of income receivers in three stages.

1. Assume that there will be no change in production on the farms as a result of the reform. Estimate the amount of redistribution that will take place from former landowners to new landowners. Estimate the amount of this income which the former landowner (a) would have saved and (b) would have spent on imports. Make the same estimates for the new owner.

2. Assume that production will increase on the redistributed land. Assume also that the production increase implies a rise in income for the new owner; that is, that production goes up more than costs. Assume that this increase is a result of the agrarian reform, and not simply a result of an increased profitability in farming. Then, on the basis of an estimate of a

marginal propensity to save for the new landowners, reestimate the savings and imports of this group.

3. Examine the use of savings on the part of former owners. Compare the results with the probability that the use of savings by new owners would be different. Evaluate the argument that says that savings will be used more productively in a redistribution.


## Data

Before proceeding with the above steps, it is necessary to discuss the type of data used, its source and reliability. There have been very few budget studies in Chile. Those that have been made represent only limited portions of the population. One study, aimed at estimating the behavior patterns of large landowners, was made in 1962 by Marvin Sternberg.[1] It has a number of limitations, not the least of which is its date. It is quite possible that these patterns have changed since 1962. Additionally, the landowners interviewed were only twenty in number and were selected by means of a positive response to a telephone question of willingness to cooperate. This is, however, the only existing study which gives a clue to the expenditure patterns of large landowners and it will be used here in discussions of this particular group. In gathering data on the working groups, the *asentados,* or former *inquilinos,* the present author interviewed 102 members of *asentamientos* randomly selected from the seventeen *asentamientos* of this study. These interviews obtained information on expenditures for particular items as well as on savings. For this sector of the economy, savings and investment are always equal, since the common way of saving is to buy an animal which may or may not be used as a work animal and whose value may or may not increase with its weight. Both purchases of certain kinds of goods and a marginal savings rate were estimated on the basis of these interviews. It is assumed that what matters is income and not whether the individuals are *asentados* or *inquilinos,* or even whether they are owners of small farms or workers. Comparisons are made with the few other studies available (mostly case studies) on low-income farm owners and/or workers in an attempt to validate the sample of *asentados* as representative.


## Estimation of Redistribution

We turn first to estimation of the redistribution impact of the reform. We seek to know whether or not the law is designed and administered in such a way as to effect a redistribution of income; and, if it is, which groups have gained and which have lost in the process. We then follow through step one as indicated above in estimating the effect this redistribution is likely to have on savings after the full reform is carried out.

In order to measure the potential for redistribution of the present agrarian reform law, we need to know the difference between the amount the former landowners received as interest on land payments and what they would have received as profits from the farm. If there is little difference in these two figures, or if, indeed, the interest paid is greater than the profits they would have received, then we conclude that there has been no redistribution from landowner to *asentado*. If, in this case, the *asentados* received more in cash than they otherwise would have been paid, we conclude that there is a redistribution from somewhere else in the economy and/or from international sources to the *asentados*. In fact during the three-year period of grace in which land payments are made by CORA, but not by *asentados*, there must be a transfer of resources from somewhere else in the economy to the *asentados* unless the share of profits paid to CORA is sufficient to pay for land payments as well as CORA administrative costs. If, on the other hand, the amount in interest payments is less than the amount of profit the farmer would have made, then there is at least some redistribution from the former owner in favor of the *asentado*.

Several assumptions must be made before we can make any calculations. Assume for the moment that income and costs would have been the same under the former management as under the *asentamiento*. (This assumption is based on the conclusion of the last chapter that there is little evidence of overall change in the production on these farms. There is no way of knowing what the costs would have been had the farms not been transferred.) Then the amount left after subtracting a charge for depreciation is equal to what would have been the wage paid to the *asentados* plus the profit of the farm. We are then left with the problem of how to estimate the wage the *asentados* would have received had the former owner still been in control. Since this estimate is crucial to the consideration of income changes on the part of *asentados* it will be discussed in detail.

One way to estimate the amount an *asentado* would have been paid is simply to express in real terms the amount he was paid before the expropriation, and assume that he would be paid the same now if the situation had remained unchanged. There is both a practical and a theoretical problem connected with this approach. The practical problem is that data on exactly the amount paid in cash as well as in kind are available for only some of the *asentamientos* in the sample. (*Asentados* simply did not remember these details from two or three years ago.) The theoretical problem is a result of the changes in legal regulation of the agricultural wage and other changes which have affected wages in the two years between the time of the expropriation and the time of the study. What is necessary is to compare what the *asentados* would have received the same year of the study if the farm were still under its former owner.

The minimum daily wage for rural workers is dictated by law, as is the percentage of this wage which must be paid in cash. Between 1965, when most of the farms in the sample were expropriated, and 1967, the year of the study, not only was the minimum wage increased from 75 to 100%—the percentage had increased in 1965 from the previous year's 50%. There is reason to expect, then, that payment in kind might have ceased entirely on the farms under consideration. In this case, it would not be accurate simply to express the combination of payments in 1965 in terms of current prices and use this as the amount that would have been received as wages in 1967.

On the other hand, there are reasons to expect that payments in kind would not have been discontinued. Because many farms have come to the attention of CORA as a result of labor unrest, and because at least one farm was expropriated after a prolonged strike, farm owners may have felt they would simply have to continue all payments in kind at their previous level and increase the cash payment to that required by law.

In an attempt to study the question of changes in the mix of payments, Pablo Ramirez of ICIRA conducted a series of interviews in 1966 with both administrators and workers in 100 large farms in the Central Valley of Chile.[2] The hypothesis of this study was that as the required percentage of wage to be paid in cash increased from 25 to 75% during the years 1953–1965, there would have been a decline in the absolute amount of payments in kind. The evidence does not strongly support the hypothesis. With respect to use of land received as part payment, 18% of those interviewed had received a decrease, but another 18% had received an increase in the amount. For pasture rights, 14% reported a decrease and 15% reported an increase in the number of animals for which they received the right of pasture. However, in regard to payments in kind of consumables such as bread, beans, milk, and firewood, although 32% registered no change, 23% received less; an additional 15% received a change in composition which was regarded as a decrease.

Table 6–1 shows the change in the minimum wage since 1955. The last column expresses the absolute amounts of the minimum wage which correspond to percentages required in cash in constant escudos of 1965. It can be seen that the most drastic changes have occurred since 1963. It is possible that changes in some of the components of noncash wages required a certain amount of time, and that the adjustments had not yet been made at the time of the study by ICIRA in 1966.

CORA preexpropriation data indicate that for those farms for which they have wage information, actual cash payments were always very close to the minimum legal cash requirement. There was always a great deal of variation in payments in kind, but cash payments tended to be consistent. In this particular study, we are interested in the agricultural year 1966–1967. On the basis of the foregoing considerations, the following assumptions are made about what wages would have been in that year. Payments in cash are assumed to have been the minimum allowed by the law. Payments in consumption goods would have been negligible; that is, they would have decreased from their previous level. And payments in land use and

**Table 6–1**

**Minimum Wage Requirements and Required Percentage to Be Paid in Cash**

| Year | Minimum Daily Wage ($E^0$) | Percent to Be Paid in Cash | Value of Required Cash Payment in Constant $E^0$, 1965 |
|---|---|---|---|
| 1955–1956 | 0.20 | 25 | 170.88 |
| 1956–1957 | 0.29 | 25 | 153.56 |
| 1957–1958 | 0.38 | 25 | 146.32 |
| 1958–1959 | 0.44 | 25 | 134.93 |
| 1959–1960 | 0.634 | 25 | 146.77 |
| 1960–1961 | 0.70 | 25 | 151.10 |
| 1961–1962 | 0.89 | 25 | 186.58 |
| 1962–1963 | 0.95 | 25 | 180.00 |
| 1963–1964 | 1.35 | 35 | 239.13 |
| 1964–1965 | 2.04 | 50 | 346.41 |
| 1965–1966 | 3.264 | 75 | 660.96 |
| 1966–1967 | 4.04 | 75 | |
| 1967 | 4.80 | 100 | |

Source: Pablo Ramirez, *Cambio en Las Formas de Pago a la Mano de Obra Agricola* (Santiago: ICIRA, 1968), p. 32.

grazing rights would have remained unchanged from the situation prior to expropriation.

In 1966–1967, the amount of cash payment required was E°3.08 per day. However, in January 1967, minimum wage legislation was changed to apply from January to January instead of from April to April. The amount to be paid in cash was then E°4.80 which was 100% of the minimum daily wage. There is an additional cost of the employers' share of the social security payments. In practice, this share is based, not on the actual wage, if payments in cash and kind are fully evaluated, but on the minimum daily wage. This adds E°1.57 per day from May 1 to January 1, and E°1.82 from January 1 to the following May. In almost every case on the *asentamientos,* the accustomed use of house, garden plot, pasture rights, and firewood were unchanged from the previous ownership structure and were not evaluated. These benefits will therefore not be added to the cost of labor. (The valuation of these items would also have to be added to the income of the farm and would, therefore, cancel out in the calculations to be made.) An allowance must be made, however, for the small portion of land received by many *inquilinos* in the regular rotation of the farm. On the basis of estimates (from other studies on wage payments) of the average rental value of this land, an allowance of E°1.80 per day was made for the land which *asentados* would have used under the former system of ownership.[3] After making all these adjustments, the average cost per worker is E°7 per day's work. This figure cannot be compared with the costs estimated by other authors since it does not include estimates of housing, etc., because of the reasons discussed.

In order to show more clearly the types of calculations used for each of the concepts, detailed calculations made on the *asentamiento* used for the case study in Chapter 4 are shown below.

The balance sheet shows a gross income of E°762,466. Direct costs, including labor costs to non-*asentados* are E°517,029. Gross profit is then E°245,437. The following calculations were made:

| | |
|---|---|
| Gross income: | E°762,466 |
| Costs | 517,029 |
| Gross profit | 245,437 |
| Depreciation | 32,234 |
| Net profit (includes *asentado* income) | 213,203 |

Depreciation is calculated by taking 5% of infrastructure and 10% of other capital. No depreciation allowance was made for land. The family allowance, paid out to *asentados* and counted as a cost in *asentamiento* bookkeeping, is added back in. This is done for two reasons. The figures will be used to estimate the income the former owner would have received. Because the government, not the owner, pays this allowance, it would not have been a cost had the land not changed hands. Secondly, in considering the figures simply as profit calculations for the *asentamiento* as a firm, this allowance should not be counted as a cost.

| | |
|---|---|
| Add to above: | E° 25,384 |
| Adjusted net profit | E°238,587 |

There are 44 *asentados* on this farm. Allowing for E°7 per day for 270 days for the year gives the imputed cost of the labor of the *asentados*. There may be some dispute about using this number instead of the actual number of days worked. But because there was considerable evidence that the number of days worked by *asentados* was overstated, the figure 270, considered to be the number of annual working days for a farm worker on full time, was used. On this basis, then, the opportunity cost of labor for the *asentamiento* is estimated at E°83,160, which leaves the return to capital and technical assistance put forth by CORA at E°155,427. This final figure, in E° of 1967, is an estimate based on the assumptions stated above of the net income the former owner would have received, and would include not only return to capital, but also return to management. Only a certain portion of this amount, however, can be attributed to the land and constructions which belonged to the former owner. The total capital of this farm is distributed as follows:

|  |  |
|---|---|
| Acquisition costs including improvements | E° 1,177,073 |
| Infrastructure and other fixed capital furnished by CORA | 203,833 |
| Machinery, tools, and livestock | 220,443 |
| Circulating capital equal to one-half operating costs plus opportunity costs of *asentado* labor | 287,402 |

Then Net Profit/Total Capital is equal to 8.2%. Or, if we revalue capital on the assumption that its value increases according to the index for the cost of living, that is, by approximately 20%, then the Net Profit/Total Capital is equal to 6.9%.

This particular farm was expropriated under the law of 1962. Because, under this law, payment to the former owner was, in most cases, equal to full value of the land, there cannot be said to have been a redistribution of income from owner to landowner. This statement is based on the assumption that there are alternative uses for capital which will earn a return equal to that earned through ownership of land. It has been said that the landowners received some income in the form of status by owning a farm. This part of the income, if indeed it existed, cannot be measured. If entrance to farming were competitive, we would expect, in equilibrium, that this status income would equal the difference between the income earned in farming and income that could be earned from alternative investments. If entrance to farming were restrictive, then the imputed value of status would be greater than the difference between alternative incomes. Only in this case would there have been a redistribution of income from landowners to workers under the 1962 law.

If this particular *asentamiento* had been expropriated under the terms of payment of the 1967 law, the owner would have received 10% of the E°1,177.073 in cash. On the assumption that he could get an equal return for both the working capital he would have invested and the 10% cash payment, and on the further assumption that output and costs would have been similar to what they were on the *asentamiento,* the income lost would have been equal to the rate of profit, 6.9%, applied to 90% of E°1,177,073, or E°72,096 in E° of 1967. This amount must now be compared with the return paid to the landowner of the remaining 90% of the value of his capital.

The method for paying back the bonds was described in Chapter 2. A 2.5% real interest rate on 70% of the capital and a −17% (20% inflation rate less the 3% nominal interest) on the remaining 30% of the capital gives a real interest rate on the total capital (that is, 90% of the original valuation) of −3.6%. The total amount of income that would have been redistributed, then, is E°72,096 − (−38,136) which is equal to E°110,232.

Similar calculations for the entire set of 17 *asentamientos* of the study give the results found in Table 6–2. On the third *asentamiento* an adjustment was made because it was felt that the costs were excessive and thus would not have represented the costs of the former owner. Problems associated with this particular *asentamiento* and its coordinator led to the conclusion that these excesses were, indeed, characteristic of the *asentamiento,* and would not have been true of the former owner.

The total amount which would have been redistributed in these 17 *asentamientos,* if they had been subject to the 1967 law, was equal to E°709,942. It is useful to express this figure in the amount redistributed per *asentado.* This latter amount is E°1,130. If we use this figure as an estimate of the probable redistributive impact of the law as it stands, we can, by using various assumptions about the number of *asentados* which will be involved, make estimates of this effect on the sector as a whole, and ask to what degree it can effect shifts in demand or savings.

In Chapter 5 we used the figure 40,000 to approximate the number of *asentados* there would be by 1971. Using this same figure here gives about E°45 million which would be redistributed annually if the number of *asentados* did not increase after 1970. If the goal of 100,000 *asentados* were reached, then over E°100 million would be redistributed. Even this amount in equivalent to less than 5% of income originating in agriculture. It is quite possible, however, that the amount of money to be redistributed per *asentado* will increase after 1968. Chapter 5 showed that there is some evidence that the lands being expropriated now were already more intensively farmed than were those of earlier expropriations. If this is true, then a greater amount per *asentado* will be redistributed in the future. A doubling of the amount redistributed per *asentado* together with a settlement of 100,000 *asentados* would affect about 10% of the income originating in agriculture. It is doubtful, however, that under the present law there would be a doubling of the redistribution, since many of the farms in the sample, as seen in Table 6–2, already have high profit rates.

### Estimation of Savings of Asentados

In this section, the assumptions and methods of the estimation of the marginal savings rate of *asentados* are explained.

*Data*

The information for this estimate is all based on the set of interviews with *asentados* made by the present author. In view of the fact that *asentados* kept no records of expenses, the answers to a questionnaire on

# Table 6-2

## Calculations of Profit and Redistribution for Seventeen Asentamientos

| Item | Asentamientos | | | | | | | | |
|---|---|---|---|---|---|---|---|---|---|
| | 1 | 2 | 3 | 4 | 5 | 6 | 7 | 8 | 9 |
| Gross income | E⁰671,633 | E⁰304,303 | E⁰358,566 | E⁰170,760 | E⁰259,011 | E⁰158,394 | E⁰762,466 | E⁰488,238 | E⁰411,229 |
| Costs | 422,831 | 136,154 | 225,031 | 84,125 | 128,571 | 88,798 | 517,029 | 258,774 | 292,739 |
| Depreciation | 31,005 | 59,667 | 24,434 | 30,719 | 17,935 | 17,311 | 32,234 | 43,229 | 26,816 |
| Family allowance [a] | 21,786 | 25,337 | 0 | 0 | 7,982 | 6,509 | 25,384 | 20,033 | 16,180 |
| Net profit | 239,583 | 133,819 | 109,101 | 55,916 | 120,487 | 58,794 | 238,587 | 206,268 | 107,854 |
| Opportunity labor costs | 58,590 | 60,380 | 15,120 | 32,130 | 39,672 [b] | 34,122 [b] | 83,160 | 134,022 [b] | 30,240 |
| Return to capital and management | 180,992 | 73,439 | 93,981 | 23,786 | 80,815 | 24,672 | 155,427 | 72,246 | 77,614 |
| Acquisition cost | 547,288 | 531,096 | 487,422 | 325,000 | 80,584 | 243,928 | 1177,073 | 1092,515 | 578,300 |
| Infrastructure | 262,182 | 536,866 | 237,940 | 296,051 | 86,228 | 90,001 | 203,833 | 650,061 | 127,620 |
| Machinery, tools, livestock | 178,534 | 29,477 | 126,352 | 153,451 | 136,242 | 128,113 | 220,443 | 107,264 | 202,891 |
| Circulating capital | 229,818 | 85,648 | 120,066 | 58,127 | 80,130 | 58,205 | 287,402 | 186,381 | 153,399 |
| Net profit/capital adjusted for inflation | (12.4%) | (5.2%) | (7.7%) | (2.4%) | (17.6%) | (4.0%) | (6.9%) | (3.0%) | (6.1%) |
| Imputed owner income | 61,077 | 24,855 | 33,778 | 7,020 | 12,764 | 8,781 | 72,096 | 29,497 | 31,748 |
| Actual owner income | −17,732 | −17,207 | −15,792 | −10,930 | −2,611 | −7,903 | −39,136 | −36,397 | −18,736 |
| Amount of redistribution | 78,808 | 42,062 | 49,570 | 17,950 | 15,375 | 16,684 | 111,232 | 65,894 | 50,484 |

# Table 6-2—Continued

| Item | Asentamientos | | | | | | | | Total |
| --- | --- | --- | --- | --- | --- | --- | --- | --- | --- |
| | 10 | 11 | 12 | 13 | 14 | 15 | 16 | 17 | |
| Gross income | E° 496,802 | E° 335,328 | E° 113,187 | E° 97,091 | E° 127,209 | E° 590,291 | E° 1015,375 | E° 605,020 | E° 6964,903 |
| Costs | 320,506 | 201,222 | 74,097 | 51,349 | 96,302 | 190,761 | 788,561 | 342,989 | 4279,839 |
| Depreciation | 32,226 | 6,006 | 23,958 | 10,862 | 18,234 | 48,109 | 86,347 | 79,877 | 588,967 |
| Family allowance a | 31,651 | 0 | 9,976 | 14,921 | 26,661 | 0 | 0 | 0 | 206,420 |
| Net profit | 175,721 | 128,100 | 25,108 | 49,801 | 39,334 | 351,421 | 140,467 | 182,154 | 2362,513 |
| Opportunity labor costs | 62,370 | 56,700 | 20,790 | 37,800 | 85,050 | 226,800 | 79,380 | 184,000 | 1240,326 |
| Return to capital and management | 113,351 | 71,400 | 4,318 | 12,001 | −45,716 | 124,621 | 61,087 | −1,843 | 1122,187 |
| Acquisition costs | 368,872 | 130,196 | 268,584 | 315,372 | 461,003 | 665,932 | 1755,751 | 808,843 | 9837,759 |
| Infrastructure | 121,769 | 21,391 | 62,063 | 60,530 | 23,166 | 113,214 | 375,803 | 126,481 | 3395,199 |
| Machinery, tools livestock | 261,386 | 49,368 | 207,545 | 78,365 | 170,760 | 424,490 | 685,574 | 720,387 | 3880,642 |
| Circulating capital | 175,612 | 128,961 | 42,455 | 37,114 | 77,345 | 208,780 | 434,470 | 263,494 | 2627,407 |
| Net profit/capital adjusted for inflation | (10%) | (18.1%) | (0.6%) | (2.0%) | (−5.2%) | (7.4%) | (1.6%) | (−0.9%) | (9.5%) |
| Imputed owner income | 33,198 | 21,091 | 1,334 | 5,676 | −21,574 | 44,359 | 25,282 | −5,828 | 385,146 |
| Actual owner income | −15,271 | −4,216 | −8,702 | −10,218 | −14,936 | −21,576 | −56,886 | −26,207 | −324,796 |
| Amount of redistribution | 48,469 | 25,307 | 10,036 | 15,894 | −6,638 | 65,927 | 82,168 | 20,379 | 709,942 |

a This amount is added back in. In the original figures it is counted as cost.
b On these *asentamientos*, opportunity cost of labor includes payment to family members additional to the *asentados* who worked on the farm. Profit shares on these, but not on other farms were calculated in the accounts on the basis of the number of days worked by the *asentado* plus other members of his family.

expenditures are subject to some error. However, there are several mitigating factors which enabled the author to feel confident that the errors are not too large. In most cases, rural families at the worker level in Chile are paid by the month and make purchases of food and clothing by the month. Durable goods are normally purchased on the installment plan or by money obtained through sale of an animal. Furthermore, monthly expenditure on food for a given *asentado* was fairly regular.

The interview procedure, therefore, was to obtain an estimate of the amount of money spent on food per month. In addition to the monthly supply of basic foods, some families bought meat once or twice a week, so a separate estimate was obtained for this item when it was purchased outside the regular monthly purchases. In most cases, the only meat eaten by *asentados* was chicken which they grew themselves. No estimate was made of this consumption of home-grown products. An attempt was made to distinguish expenditures during the winter and summer months, since it was felt that there would be more cash expenditure during the winter than during the summer. This was not often the case, however, since in the winter rural families and also urban worker families simply do without vegetables which they have not dried and stored themselves. Annual food purchases were based on monthly purchases adjusted for differences in winter and summer months where necessary.

For clothing, the procedure was to list the items purchased during the year for each member of the family separately. A family could never estimate how much money was spent on clothing in a year, but the family (usually the mother) almost always remembered the number as well as the price of shoes, dresses, etc., purchased for each member of the family in a year.

Durable goods were in most cases easy to remember. The interview procedure was to ask whether or not certain items were owned by the family and whether they were purchased in the last year. If so, the price was obtained. Questions were asked on a list of items which *asentados* might be expected to want. All common household items were included.

Other expenses and purchases, such as fuel, education, liquor, cigarettes, transportation, were itemized as separate estimates. In all cases the method was to obtain an estimate on a daily, weekly, or monthly basis, depending on how the family made its purchases. For example, in the case of education, it was ascertained how many children were in school and the approximate expenditure on each one for books, etc. In no case is actual tuition charged, but in most cases a very small monthly sum was paid into the equivalent of a fathers' club.

The family was then asked for an inventory of animals owned privately, the number purchased and sold during the year. The net change in inventory constitutes most of the savings of these families. No attempt was made to estimate increased value through gaining of weight over the year since no evaluations of this type were made by *asentados*. This procedure underestimates both income and savings. Strictly speaking, the increased value through the gaining of weight less the cost of feeding the animal that year is an addition to income. If the animal is not sold in that year, there is an addition to savings by the same amount. Animal sales were treated as decreases in assets, thus ignoring the part of this sale which was income. In most cases, for the type of animals bought by *asentados,* this error was probably not large. This type of saving is potentially quite significant. If *asentados* were taught to save in some other form, such as savings accounts, reinvested interest could be quite important.

The other source of investment was in the purchase of tools and even, in one case, a tractor by individual *asentados*. These tools were for use on the garden plots, and, in some cases, were purchased with a view toward future ownership of parcels.

Finally, questions were asked to ascertain if and how much the family might be in debt. This debt would be in the form of payments still to be made on installment plan purchases. It is interesting to note that no *asentado,* when asked about debt, included the advances made by CORA, even when advances from the previous year had not been paid. The awareness of this debt became apparent only in the initial reluctance of some *asentados* to speak about their animal inventories. These *asentados* feared that CORA would take the animals in lieu of debt payment.

Since there was an exact record of how much cash advance each *asentado* actually received, income was not too difficult to determine with accuracy. There is some error in the estimates possible, however, when given by those *asentados* who made cash sales of products from their garden plots.

The amount of cash an *asentado* had to spend (cash advances, share in profits, sales of products, plus the family allowance), in addition to the debts contracted during the year as well as dissaving through animal sales, was used as a check on the reliability of the expenditure estimates. In all cases it was assumed that the estimates of available cash were correct since there was much less possibility of error.

In no case was there a very large discrepancy between the amount of money that an *asentado* was supposed to have and the amount of money he said he used either in consumption or in purchases of animals and tools. Since there was reason to believe that most of the error was in the food estimate, this item was usually adjusted in such a way as to make total expenditure equal total cash available plus debt. In some cases the adjustment was made in clothing, particularly where an *asentado* seemed a little unsure in this area.

*Assumptions*

In the determination of a household consumption function, it was assumed that advances were regarded as income and that no account was taken as to whether or not the farm would make sufficient profits to pay off the advances. Income from products sold, the family allowance, and the year-end share of profits (when these were positively in excess of advances made during the year) were also counted as income. Only cash advances were counted. *Asentados* were able to purchase some types of durable goods, animals, seed for garden plots, and even food on credit from the *asentamiento*. These purchases were simply added to the amount that the *asentado* owed CORA at the end of the year. They were deducted from the share of profits which were to go to each *asentado*. Again in this case, if profits did not cover both cash advances and these credits, the debt was simply carried over to the next year.

Strictly speaking, if cash advances are treated as income by *asentados* it might be argued that imputed values for all types of advances should be counted. Imputed value of consumed home production should also be counted. Then expenditure would include all the consumption, not only of cash expenditures, but also of these other products. One would expect that the amount of this income in kind available for consumption would affect the savings rate out of cash income. The following justification is offered for not counting these other types of income and expenditures.

In the first place, the goal here is simply to obtain some rough estimate of the order of magnitude of the average and marginal propensity to save out of cash income. It was felt that year-to-year variations in the production available for consumption from the garden plots is not great. Therefore, the effects of this production would not cause much year-to-year variation in the propensity to save out of cash income. The fact that estimation of this type of production and consumption would be highly unreliable would, in any case, create perhaps more inaccuracies than it solved. Consumption goods in kind sold on credit to *asentados* was quite small, so these were not counted. Durable goods and investment goods received on credit from the *asentamiento* were treated as all other durable goods and investment goods. The item was considered an expenditure (or investment), and if it were not paid for at the end of the year, the value was considered debt. If the profits were sufficient to cover the debt, then this amount was also counted as income.

The most important assumption for econometric purposes is that savings is truly a residual and that random fluctuations in consumption are always matched by opposite random fluctuations in savings. In more formal terms this assumption implies that the error term in the equation

$$C = a + bY + e$$

is negatively correlated with changes in savings. This assumption seems plausible for the particular cross section of families with which we are concerned. In cross-section samples where investment is considered to have an independent distribution, a simultaneous model would have to be solved; but at this low level of income it is argued that the method of savings always involves investment directly and that it is always a residual.

*Methodology*

Ordinary least squares regression was used to estimate the marginal propensity to consume using the definitions of income and consumption given above. In addition to a simple model using only one independent variable, income, other independent variables were tested in the equation. An attempt was also made to estimate income elasticities for various types of durable goods, but, as we shall see, these attempts led to rather unsatisfactory results.

*Results*

The following results were obtained in the regressions used to estimate savings rates and income elasticity for durable goods.

*Family consumption*

$$C = 1586 + 0.66Y$$
$$(395) \quad (0.07) \qquad \bar{R}^2 = 0.46$$

where

$C$ = consumption of the family
$Y$ = family disposable income as defined earlier

and

$$C = 2.8 + 0.66Y$$
$$(0.57) \quad (0.07) \qquad \bar{R}^2 = 0.49$$

where

$C$ = the logarithm of family consumption
$Y$ = the logarithm of family disposable income

*Per Capita Consumption*

$$C = 107.8 + 0.82Y$$
$$(52.0) \quad (0.06) \qquad \bar{R}^2 = 0.66$$

where $C$ and $Y$ are expressed in per capita terms; and

$$C = 1243 + 0.63Y + 75.2N - 14.3D$$
$$(451) \quad (0.08) \quad (48.1) \quad (27.1) \qquad \bar{R}^2 = 0.48$$

where

$N$ = the number of persons in the family
$D$ = an estimate of the value of durable goods already owned

An estimate of the relationship between disposable income and durable goods does give a significant coefficient for disposable income even though the regression correlation is low. The following results were obtained:

$$D_n = -186 + 0.13Y - 5.97D_o$$
$$(212) \quad (0.04) \quad (14.4) \qquad \bar{R}^2 = 0.10$$

where

$$D_n = \text{new purchases of durable goods}$$
$$D_o = \text{durable goods already owned}$$

The income elasticity at the mean of new purchases of durable goods is calculated to be approximately 1.4.

The average savings of the entire group of *asentados* is about 4%. The average amount spent on durable goods was 8.5%. For most of the following section we shall use the family marginal propensity to save to be 34%.

Some check on the validity of these estimates is found by comparing them with estimates made for rural families. In the 1966 ICIRA study of 100 large farms, although a complete budget study was not attempted, estimates were made of food expenditures and of investment expenditures in animals, tools, etc. This latter figure is the equivalent of savings as defined above. The average rate for the *inquilinos* was 4.2%.[4] The income levels of these *inquilinos* are similar to the income levels of the *asentados* in this study. In a second study, that for the 1965 INPROA groups mentioned above, an average savings rate of 25% was observed for an average income almost twice as high as that for the *asentados* in the sample. If we use the above estimate of *asentados'* marginal propensity to save to calculate the amount which would be saved out of a doubled income, we get a rate of 19%. Because the INPROA group average is pushed up by an extremely high rate (59%) on one farm, it is probably somewhat exaggerated. The rate on the other three farms involved was around 17 or 18%. The rates found in the *asentado* study are fairly consistent with these two earlier studies. This lends credence to the argument that it is income that counts and not whether the family is *inquilino* or *asentado*.

For the estimates of savings of former landowners, we can use the results of the Sternberg study. Some of the farms in this study were jointly owned, and Sternberg does not follow up the budget study on all the families involved. He calculated percentages of expenditure on various items on the basis of the portion of the farm income which went to the families in his sample, after reinvested profits were deducted. This portion was about 70% of the amount distributed to families. In the following discussion it is assumed that the same percentages apply to the other families. So, while the percentages are those given by Sternberg, they are applied to the entire net profit of the farms involved. The limitations of Sternberg's study have already been cited, but no other attempt has been made to study the spending behavior of large landowners. Sternberg makes a distinction between the net profit of the farm and the personal income of the landowner. The difference between the two is profits reinvested in the farm. In the discussion which follows we refer to the redistribution of the entire net profit, which includes what Sternberg calls the personal income of the owner. His estimate of reinvested profits was 27%. Not all of this amount was invested in equally productive ways, since some portion went into the construction of farm housing for the owner. An additional 11.9% was either saved or invested outside of agriculture. Approximately 8% of the total net profit was spent on housing and 7.8% on durables including automobiles.

If the total amount paid out by CORA in advances for the seventeen *asentamientos* of the sample is subtracted from the total amount CORA received back in profit shares, the result is negative. The entire net profit on these farms, therefore, was included in personal income. The comparable figure from Sternberg is his combined production consumption unit. We first need to know whether *asentados'* marginal propensity to consume is less than, equal to, or greater than that of landowners. Although Sternberg's sample was too small to estimate a marginal propensity to consume, we can, by projecting the *asentados'* income, examine what will happen to their savings at higher income levels. Sternberg estimates disposable income per landowning family at about E°55,000.[5] In 1967 escudos this amount is approximately E°275,000. Using the consumption function estimated for *asentados* we can say that average savings at this income level would be about 33%. For the landowners in Sternberg's sample all savings were approximately 39%. The implication here is that either the marginal propensity to save is not linear, that is, it increases at higher incomes, or that landowners in general have a higher marginal propensity to save. Thus we can say that savings out of the redistributed income will be less than they otherwise would have been. On the assumption that the intercept is the same value for the consumption function of both landowners and *asentados,* we can argue that the decrease in savings out of the redistributed income can be, at most, 5%. Based on the estimate made earlier of the size of the redistribution for 40,000 *asentados,* the amount that savings could be decreased would be equal to approximately 0.1% of income originating in agriculture. Thus we argue that although the analysis leads us to expect a decline in savings, that decline is of an insignificant magnitude. This analysis tells us nothing, however, about the redistribution to *asentados* which is occurring from the other sectors in the economy.

## Expenditure on Imports

Sternberg estimates the import content of the consumption of landlords to be about 25%, which represents about 15% of net income.[6] This figure may well have decreased since 1960 because both trade policy and import substitution have changed since that time. The *asentados* had no expenditure on items which would have been imported. Whether or not this is significant is determined by the degree to which Chile's expansion is dependent on foreign exchange. Mamalakis makes a case for such dependence.[7] He argues that the reason the inflation in Chile has not resulted in a flight to the capital goods sector is that, given Chile's size, such a sector is uneconomic. If this interpretation is correct, then capital imports are necessary for expansion. Therefore imports for consumption, by using up foreign exchange, deter expansion. Unfortunately, we cannot estimate an income elasticity of demand for imported consumer goods from Sternberg's figures. We cannot be certain, then, of the impact of income redistribution on such imports. If the elasticity is high, as we would expect, then a considerable amount of imports would be affected. Using Sternberg's average income to landlords and the amount per landlord redistributed, we can say that for those landlords affected, income would be decreased about 10% to 13%. An income elasticity of two, for example, could decrease their expenditures on imports by 20 to 26%.

### Demand for Domestic Industrial Products

It would appear from the estimation of the amount of redistribution that demand for domestic products could not be strongly affected. When we examine the aggregate production of some industries involved, this impression is confirmed.

From the results of the estimation of expenditure on durable goods out of disposable income we can say that approximately 13% of an increase in income will be spent for durable goods. The majority of the items involved here can be classified as furniture, kitchen appliances, radios, and sewing machines. These items were grouped because there was no significant correlation with income when taken separately. Using again the redistribution figure of E°45 million, we estimate expenditures on durable goods out of this redistribution at E°5.9 million. From 1966 manufacturing census data we have figures for gross output in various industries.[8] The classifications involved here are those for furniture, electrical appliances, and metal products. Gross output in E° of 1967 for these three census classifications are as follows:

|  |  |
|---|---|
| Furniture | E°   84 million |
| Electrical appliances | 332 million |
| Metal products | 704 million |
| Total | E°1120 million |

The increased expenditure on these products as a result of the redistribution from landlord to *asentado* cannot affect output very much even with no decline in the purchase of these goods by landlords whose income has decreased.

There is a serious aggregation problem here. It is quite possible that with smaller breakdowns the amount of expenditure by *asentados* relative to total output would be significant. Furthermore, it is highly probable that expenditure elasticities for these products will be higher as income reaches a slightly higher level. With the information at our disposal, however, we are left with the conclusion that the redistribution from the landowner to *asentado* is probably not large enough to affect demand for domestically produced industrial goods.

### Reestimation of Savings with Increased Farm Income

Although the evidence so far available does not indicate a significant increase in production on the *asentamientos,* such increases may in fact occur after a few years' experience. If, for example, there were a 20% increase in production on *asentamientos,* will any of the conclusions in the above section be affected? Calculating a 20% increase over the base of the return to capital and management estimated earlier gives an additional E°350 per *asentado.* We must make some assumption about CORA's behavior relative to such an increase; and it is a fair assumption that most of the increase would be on farms where "profits" are already positive. Therefore, unless CORA changes its policy with regard to such "profits," about 90% of the increase will go to *asentados.* If there were significant increases on *asentamientos* which now have negative "profits," most of the increase would probably go to CORA to pay debts. The application of the marginal savings rate to the increase per *asentado,* E°315 (90% of E°350), gives an additional E°117 per *asentado* saved. On the assumption that this increased income is a result of the reform itself, the savings increase here is net. Nevertheless, the amount involved is still quite small relative to total agricultural income.

These calculations can be made on other assumptions which lead to different conclusions. If the farms now being expropriated are more representative of the total farm universe than those previously expropriated, we can calculate a 20% increase on the base of the total income originating in agriculture. In Chapter 5 we stated that on the basis of a given amount of land per *asentado,* the *asentamientos* would control about 10% of the agricultural land in Chile (including 10% of the irrigated land). On this basis an increase of 20% on *asentamientos* could increase total agricultural production by 2%. Income originating in agriculture includes payment to all factors, but if we assume that all income receivers will save at least 30% of the increase in income we can argue that total savings out of agricultural income would increase by about 0.6%.

There are further ramifications of such an increase in production. Even without assuming a higher income elasticity for durable goods at this higher income level, the increase in production assumed here would double the expenditure on durable goods estimated earlier. The total increase in expenditure on durable goods, therefore, would be equal to about 1% of the total gross output in the three industries for which we calculated totals. Of course, the 1% is calculated on the size of these industries in 1966, and the level of increase in production we are talking about is based on the number of *asentados* projected for 1971. Growth in the industries between 1966 and 1971 would make this percentage lower. Nevertheless, it is not unreasonable to believe that, given the amount of aggregation involved, the percent of the sales for the relevant disaggregated industries would be significant. However, whether or not an increase in demand of, say, 5% in a given industry would lead to innovation, depends on the structure of the industry. Information about the structure of these industries is not now available, but a closer examination of this kind of data is necessary before it can be assumed that investment in mass-produced goods would be stimulated by this level of demand.

Another ramification of an increase in production of 20% on *asentamientos* is the import saving on agricultural production. This amount saved in imports would not be equivalent to the 20% increase in production, however, since there would be some increase in demand for food on the part of *asentados*.

## Use of Savings

Although use of savings may well be the most important aspect of a redistribution, not very much can be said here. In his thesis, Sternberg does not quantify the amount of investment in foreign exchange, housing, etc. He classifies consumption but not investment expenditures. CIDA quotes Sternberg in a classification of the investment data which went into agriculture. Since Sternberg was on the CIDA committee he presumably used this more detailed breakdown for the CIDA report even though he does not present it in his thesis. From the information given in CIDA it is possible to calculate that about 20% of farm investment was spent on construction.[9] Most of this construction is probably housing. Sternberg states that the investment outside of agriculture went into either urban real estate or stocks and bonds. He does not specify the form in which savings were held, but it is probable that they were held in the form of dollars. The savings component was about 5% of total savings.

The maximum amount of "nonproductive" investment was 40% of total savings. The actual amount is probably closer to 25%.

We can ask if this situation will be different for the redistributed income. At the present time most *asentado* savings is in the form of animal purchases. In the near future, however, the residual from consumption will probably not exceed that required to make housing and land payments. The latter are in turn passed on to the landlords. The housing payments, it is true, can be used by the government, at the time they are repaid, to finance directly productive investment; but it must be remembered that the original investment was, in fact, housing. Additional savings by *asentados* in the form of animal purchases cannot be transferred to the rest of the economy unless some mechanism is developed to rechannel these savings.

## Conclusion

This chapter has defined some of the factors that must be considered when land redistribution is viewed as a means to redistribute income and thereby stimulate demand for the products of domestic industry. Given the small size of the rural relative to the urban population in Chile, a very large amount of redistribution would be required to have a noticeable effect on the demand for industrial products. On the assumption that the amount of redistribution of future *asentamientos* will be the same as that for present ones, it is doubtful that any effect on such demand could be felt. There are two ways, however, that the redistribution of future expropriations could be greater. One of these is a higher inflation rate. Though not advocated here, the higher the rate of inflation, the greater the amount of redistribution. The second way is through the expropriation of farms which, prior to expropriation, were more profitably operated than those in the sample studied. In the event of the occurrence of either of these two possibilities, an impact on the demand for industrial products could be felt. In other words, the agrarian reform law is, in fact, written in such a way that it can effect a reasonably large income redistribution.

# 7 Ideal Versus Reality

Thus far we have discussed the possible effects of Chile's agrarian reform on the basis of its present mode of operation. In this chapter we point out some of the problems associated with the present operation of CORA and suggest improvements that might better accomplish the goals of the reform.

## Organization of CORA

The reform has become a strong political issue in the sense that one's loyalty to the Christian Democratic Party is questioned if one is at all critical of the reform. This fact, among others, has caused confusion in the organizational structure of CORA. The confusion takes the form of conflicting goals which result in conflicting pressures brought to bear upon decision makers within the organizational structure. Before stating some examples of these conflicts, a description of the general structural organization of CORA is in order. As in all government agencies in Chile, the nominal president of CORA is the president of the Republic. Operationally speaking, however, the final decision-making power is in the hands of the vice-president of CORA. Chile is divided into twelve geographic regions, or zones, each of which has a director. Each zone is, in turn, divided into several areas with a director in each area. Each zonal office has a staff of accountants, technical experts in agricultural engineering, social service experts, construction experts, and purchasing and distributing agents. A description of the actual process of expropriation will show where the basic decision-making powers lie. The central CORA office in Santiago decides each year on the number of families to be organized into *asentamientos*. This office then assigns a proportion of this number to be settled in each of the zones. It is then the job of each zonal office to decide which farms will be expropriated and formed into *asentamientos*. The zonal office has on file information on the size and value of all farms in the zone, which information was obtained from the project air-photograph of 1965 and from the internal revenue office. Agricultural engineers are making a systematic effort to visit all farms larger than 80 standard hectares to obtain information on the current and potential use of the land, the number of laborers, the infrastructure, etc. The zonal office must decide how many farms to expropriate in a given year in order to settle the number of families which has been set as the goal. Many potentially expropriable farms come to the attention of the CORA office through committees of workers on the farm who make complaints about their treatment. The specific farms to be expropriated are decided upon by the zonal director and staff, but these expropriations are subject to the approval of the central CORA office. For each farm to be expropriated, the zonal director must send to the central office all the basic information and state the reason for expropriation. The final decision on each farm rests with the central office.

After the decision to expropriate a farm has been made, further studies are carried out and a plan of land use and rotational cycle is prepared by the technical personnel. Infrastructure needs are surveyed and work is begun on fulfilling these needs soon after the farm is expropriated. Decisions on farm management and construction are made at the zonal level within the budget limits set for the zone by the central office. The zonal office acts as both a purchasing agent for inputs and a distributing agent for sales.

Even though a plan of land use is prepared by the technical experts of CORA, the actual decisions on just what is planted is in the hands of the administrative committee of the *asentamiento*. There are two CORA officials on the seven-man administrative committee. Although able to influence policy, these officials are not able to insist on a certain course of action. If the plan prepared by the technical experts is not the same as that prepared by the committee, the former is simply dropped. Since detailed plans for each farm are prepared by these experts, it is clear that, unless they are used, a great deal of expensive time is wasted in their preparation.[a] The desire to plan and control production (resulting from CORA's overall objective to increase production) is in conflict with the desire to allow autonomy and to promote "learning by doing" at the local level. And herein lies one of the most serious sources of conflicting pressures.

The broader conflict between the political goal of making the reform popular in every aspect, and the economic goal of having an efficient organizational structure and making productive use of the budget, shows up in various ways. One example of local versus central decision making based on political motivation can be seen in the regulations regarding visitors to *asentamientos*. In early 1968 a regulation was made that no one was to be allowed either to question *asentamiento* members or to receive any kind of information from the coordinator of the *asentamiento* without the prior consent of the central CORA office, the zonal office, and the area office. In one of this author's visits to *asentamientos,* the area office head telephoned the zonal office long distance because the permission to visit was not in writing.

A more serious example of the conflict between political goals and the efficient use of resources is found in the program of house building on *asentamientos*. On practically all the expropriated farms, the houses of

---

[a] The author spent some time discussing this issue with one of the experts involved. This engineer was frustrated and was considering leaving CORA. The main reason for the frustration was that he felt that if the plans he worked to prepare continued to be ignored, his job was useless.

resident laborers are in poor condition. On many *asentamientos,* one of the largest expenditures of money is in the construction of a new house for each of the resident laborers. In some cases, these are good quality, permanent houses. But discussion with a large number of the families who received these houses revealed that there was comparatively little feeling of need for them, and, indeed, among some families there was an outright preference for the former house. The money spent constructing such solid houses might well have been spent on more directly productive projects, such as the settling of more families on *asentamientos.* One great need of infrastructure is, for example, improvement of irrigation facilities and, in particular, of irrigation facility adjustments which have to be made if the land is to be parceled. Furthermore, the necessary housing, which either replaced houses completely beyond repair or was needed for families who actually had no homes of their own, could have been in the form of lower cost, temporary houses. The argument for temporary housing is based on two assumptions. The future development of the Chilean economy will probably lead to some reconsolidation and to the migration of more farm laborers to the urban-industrial centers. Thus the building of higher cost, permanent housing at this early stage shows lack of foresight. Secondly, if true human dignity is sought, then the individuals themselves should be able to supervise the building of their own homes if they are to be permanent. But since these are individuals who are not now paying for the homes, houses are built within the budget and under the direction of CORA. Two of the five zonal offices visited by the author had rather elaborate offices and equipment as well as technicians hired to prepare blueprints and to supervise the construction of these houses. It is the opinion of the author, after talking to various CORA officials, that the reason for the emphasis on house building was primarily to gain popularity by being able to advertise how many persons had received new homes. We do not wish to stress efficiency at the expense of social values. But the resources CORA has available will be either concentrated among a few receivers or spread out among a larger number. In fact, the very resources available to CORA could alternatively be used for other social expenditures.

Another example of this conflict of goals between political popularity and efficient use of resources is found in the treatment of *asentamientos* who refuse to cooperate with CORA. In the random sample of twenty farms, two could not be studied because CORA had no data. These were cases in which CORA made advances of inputs and cash subsistence allowances with the understanding that the produce of the farm would be sold through CORA, who would then keep an amount equal to the advances made during the year, and return the remainder to the *asentados.* However, on these two farms, no produce was sold through CORA and the members of the *asentamientos* simply said that there was none to sell— that production was so low that all of it was used as food for the *asentados* themselves. CORA officials knew this was not the case, that the output had been sold without marketing through CORA, and that CORA was not going to be paid back the advances.

The bad publicity which could have come from this experience was sufficient to make CORA ignore the problem. Although it is not yet clear just what will be done, there is every indication that these individuals will be allowed to continue their operation, without further advances, it is true, but also without legal action to require payment.

### The Asentamiento as an Educational Experience

The major constructive criticism this author has to make about the manner of operation of the *asentamiento* concerns its use as an educational experience. The conflicts pointed out above cannot easily be resolved. The continuance of the reform does depend upon its political acceptability, and it is not within the province of a non-Chilean to be able to say just where a particular action can be changed without losing so much acceptability as to paralyze all future actions. Nevertheless, the author does find some support for the claim that there is too much concern about the reaction of urban workers to every phase of CORA activity. The author had contact with a number of leaders of urban workers, among whom there was a growing sentiment that the government was paying too much attention to the agricultural reforms and not enough to reforms for industrial laborers who constitute a much larger percentage of the total work force.

One of the most significant aspects of the *asentamiento* as a training experience is the role of the resident coordinator.[1] There were three basic types of coordinators observed by the author in visits to *asentamientos:* those who gave advice when asked and otherwise sat in an office; those who were teacher-leaders of the type described in the case study of Chapter 4; and those who were practically a replacement of the former owner. CORA has emphasized in the training of these personnel that their role is simply that of advisor. But if it is true that *asentados* need to be taught how to be farm managers, then they must have a teacher. It is therefore, the author's contention that the role needed is that of teacher-leader. This observation is based on the fact that the three most productive *asentamientos* in the sample studied and the three with the highest amount of private capitalization among the members, had coordinators filling a teacher-leader role. A person who simply gives advice when asked could as easily live in some other place and be available to *asentamientos* by telephone. There would be no need to pay a resident advisor on each farm. A person who makes all the decisions himself is not giving the *asentados* the experience they need in decision making. But a person who knows how to influence decisions so that they are technically better, gives *asentados* experience in making decisions while at the same time teaching them better techniques. It is the opinion of the author that not only would *asentamientos* function better now, but the future farm owners would be better prepared for their positions as farm managers if the coordinators themselves were trained to be teachers. (During the same period of time in which the author was visiting the *asentamientos,* a number of Peace Corps workers who had been placed on *asentamientos* circulated a paper among CORA officials who were interested. This paper contained some of the same criticisms of this chapter, especially this criticism of the role of the coordinator.)

If the *asentamiento* is to be a learning experience there are other requirements in addition to the need for a teacher. One of these is motivation. A serious handicap in the area of motivation is the timing of the account auditing. Because the accounts of every *asentamiento* must be carefully audited in the central office in Santiago, the time required for auditing is quite long. Before *asentados* know how they stand, and before they receive their share of profits when there are profits, the audit must be received back from Santiago. It is rare that the auditing has been completed by December when the next agricultural year is more than half over. All the planning and most of the planting must have been done before December. If *asentados* are supposed to learn to be managers and to act as profit maximizers, it is essential that they have immediate feedback on whether or not there is profit.

The accounting itself also leaves something to be desired in the area of training for the future. During the *asentamiento* period, interest is not charged on circulating capital. It will be charged after the *asentamiento* period, when CORA will not give as much financial assistance. For *asentados* to accept suddenly being charged interest on subsistence loans and input loans will be very difficult.

One final criticism of the educational aspect of the *asentamiento* is the uncertainty which characterizes many phases of the operation. This criticism does not imply that the *asentados* were not clearly told about the issues involved, but rather that they were not told with sufficient emphasis to help them understand. In some cases, however, CORA officials themselves were unclear. The most important example of lack of clarity and certainty concerns the plan for future ownership of land. In the INPROA project a definite timetable was planned from the beginning. This timetable stated the manner in which the cooperative ownership would be phased into individual ownership. On the CORA farms, however, *asentados* are uncertain about the future organization. Many claim that the government is becoming the new patrón. This lack of clarity *before* the expropriation of land may well be one of the most serious obstacles to effective motivation.

Uncertainty also exists about the kinds of measures which will be taken if *asentados* do not pay their debts to CORA, for either cash advances or for purchases of animals or durable consumer goods bought on credit from

CORA. The stated policy of CORA is that these persons will be eliminated from *asentamientos*. The effectiveness of this policy is hampered by the fact that some coordinators simply advise the *asentados* not to worry about it. Furthermore, these debts are fast growing on such a scale that it may not be politically feasible to enforce the sanction.

## The Agrarian Reform and Issues of
## Social Justice

One of CORA's stated objectives for the rural worker is to equalize his opportunity for earning. To this end, *asentamientos* are supposed to adjust the number of members to the amount of land available. This adjustment has proved to be very slow in execution. Expansion of the number of *asentados* is resisted by those already present. Movement from farms with too many resident laborers is even more difficult. The author could find no evidence of systematic effort to encourage *asentados* in crowded areas to move to *asentamientos* where there was a shortage of labor. Positive incentives might be offered to encourage *asentados* to move. The failure to make such an adjustment is costly and it might be questioned to what degree other sectors of the economy should bear this cost. It would seem that at the minimum there should be a clear statement of intent made to *asentados* that $x$ number will have to move. Advertisements of available space on other *asentamientos* and clear explanation of arrangements for moving may well enable *asentados* to volunteer for other areas.

In short, both clarity of purpose and discipline are lacking in the administration of *asentamientos*. By discipline is meant the ability to confront and accept all of the responsibilities of farm management. If the *asentamiento* is to be a management-training experience these two qualities would seem to be requirements.

CORA recognizes most of these problems and is attempting to deal with them. The logistics involved in organizing this program present formidable problems and can probably be handled in time. One of the strongest grounds for optimism lies in the genuine interest of CORA officials in constant evaluation.

# 8  Costs and Alternatives

Under the supposition that there are at present few measurable benefits in production, we argue that the reform should be considered primarily as a method to redistribute income, and we must ask how much this redistribution will cost.

Before turning to the cost of the reform, some potentially quantifiable and some nonquantifiable benefits will be pointed out. It will be recalled that there was little evidence to support the hypothesis that output had increased under *asentamiento* management. It is possible that *asentados* do not really think of themselves as managers and for this reason have not yet manifested the increased effort expected of them. If parcelization succeeds in motivating such effort, then there is a possibility that net output will be increased. However, this increase in output is not yet measurable. Any eventual benefit derived from the increase in production will have to be discounted for the three or four years in which no net increase was experienced.

A second potentially quantifiable benefit is the impact on industrial production which may result from the redistribution of income. In theory, it is possible to measure the increase in industrial output that could result from such a redistribution, and in Chapter 6 it was suggested that there is reason to believe such a result might occur. Measurement of this impact would require a separate study and is not attempted here.

There is one nonquantifiable economic impact of the reform which has not yet been discussed in this paper. It is possible that a shock to the agricultural sector such as the agrarian reform law of 1967 will have long-run effects which cannot now be accurately predicted or measured. Such an argument supports a theory that the Mexican revolution created attitudinal changes that had positive effects on long-run growth.[1] Until recently in Mexico it appeared that output on the agrarian reform farms was not significantly better than output on nonreform farms. However, it is possible that the simple fact of expropriation and redistribution had effects on the attitudes of all farmers strong enough to increase long-run growth in the entire agricultural sector. At the present time there are no satisfactory ways to measure attitudinal change. If in the future it becomes possible to quantify in some way the impact of shock, then the full effects of the agrarian reform might be measured. The author's opinion is that the Chilean reform has not caused a sufficiently strong shock to expect very much in the way of long-run positive results from this particular source. The time and planning required to organize the *asentamiento* structure for three years have mitigated the shock impact, while the budget cut imposed on CORA in 1968 has slowed the process considerably. Unless the 1970 election results in an increase in political strength by those favoring a quicker and more dramatic reform, there should be little expectation of a long-run attitudinal change from the shock effect of the reform.

This author sees the increased use of idle land as perhaps the most fruitful effect of the reform. But the realization of this potential requires that CORA use its control over credit to insist on more intensive land use. CORA can also use its legal right to force evacuation if the land payments are not made. The payment for land and the repayment of loaned capital including the house built by CORA funds would require that the land be more fully utilized than it is now on most *asentamientos*. Thus, if CORA refuses titles unless payments are made regularly, there is hope for increased production. If, however, this procedure is not politically feasible, then, judging from the present behavior of *asentados,* production will probably improve very little.

The most useful way to consider the cost of the reform is to estimate the cost per family. If there are no future increases in output, then all expenditures, including those for capital, must be counted as costs of social reform. If it is expected that the capital being invested now will be paid back with interest (at some appropriate rate), then only operating costs need be considered.

Current expenses of CORA include the administrative cost of both the central and local CORA offices, as well as the payment to the coordinators of *asentamientos*. Rough estimates of annual administrative cost per *asentado* were made by dividing the total current expenses of each year by the number of *asentados* of that year. The figures for 1965–1967 were then averaged. There is evidence of some economies of scale in administration which would be expected to increase as the scale gets still larger, so the three-year average of 1965–1967 may decrease.

Capital costs include infrastructure, land acquisition, short-term financing of production, and loans for equipment and livestock. The short-term financing is supposed to be repaid at the end of the agricultural year, but these repayments, plus the profit share CORA has received, have not been sufficient to repay CORA. In 1966 and 1967 only about one-third of this short-term capital was repaid. The excess of loans over repayment must be counted as a cost. This excess was discounted by 26 percent in order to account for a 5 percent real rate of interest.

If we add all capital costs to the administrative cost, the implications for the economy are the following. For each new *asentado* incorporated into the *asentamiento,* there is a cost of E°23,000. For each *asentado* carried by CORA beyond the first year, there is a cost of E°14,800. If it is assumed that CORA will continue only the short-term loans for production during the three years post-*asentamiento* (before land payments begin), we can calculate the annual cost up to 1970 using CORA's projected increase in the number of families to be settled.

Assume that the *asentamiento* period will last only three years for those *asentados* incorporated after 1966. Assume also that CORA will incorporate 10,000 *asentados* in each of the years 1969 and 1970. Approximately this many were incorporated in 1968 even though CORA projected 15,000 for this year. Table 8–1 shows what would be, under these assumptions,

**Table 8–1**

**Projected Number of Asentados, 1968–1970**

| Year | *Asentados* (new) | *Asentados* (old) | Post-*Asentamiento* |
|------|------|------|------|
| 1968 | 10,000 | 7,000 | 1,000 |
| 1969 | 10,000 | 14,000 | 4,000 |
| 1970 | 10,000 | 20,000 | 8,000 |

the distribution of *asentados* in the two stages of *asentamiento* and post-*asentamiento* in the three years 1968, 1969, and 1970.

Two alternative cost calculations will be used. The second will assume economies of scale which reduce expenditures by $E°3,000$ per *asentado* family beginning in 1968. This assumption is based on CORA's projected budget for 1968. The costs that would be associated with these projections after 1968, together with the actual cost for the three years prior to 1968,

**Table 8–2**

**Cost Estimates in $E°1,000$'s of 1967**

| Year | First Estimate | Second Estimate (Economies of Scale) |
|------|------|------|
| 1965 | 52,311 | 52,311 |
| 1966 | 102,082 | 102,082 |
| 1967 | 181,538 | 181,538 |
| 1968 | 340,400 | 255,400 |
| 1969 | 464,400 | 344,400 |
| 1970 | 580,400 | 430,400 |

are given in Table 8–2. The cost in U.S. dollars at the official exchange rate average for 1967 is shown in Table 8–3.

In order to put these figures into perspective, it is useful to express them as a percentage of GNP. Assuming a 7% increase in GNP between 1968–1969 and 1969–1970, the cost in terms of GNP will increase from 0.4% in 1966 to 1.7% in 1970. The accuracy of these projections is not important; the main point is the cost to the economy of the agrarian reform. The amount of money invested in this project could alternatively have been used to finance other investments or other social reforms.

**Table 8–3**

**Cost Estimates in $1,000's of 1967**

| Year | First Estimate | Second Estimate (Economies of Scale) |
|------|----------------|--------------------------------------|
| 1965 | 10,462 | 10,462 |
| 1966 | 20,416 | 20,416 |
| 1967 | 36,307 | 36,307 |
| 1968 | 68,080 | 50,080 |
| 1969 | 92,880 | 68,880 |
| 1970 | 116,080 | 86,080 |

If a traditional cost-benefit analysis could be applied here, these costs could be compared with an evaluation of the benefits. At this moment, there is little evidence of benefits which can be quantified. It is for the Chilean people to decide whether or not both potential and unquantifiable benefits derived from the reform are worth this cost.

One way to determine if the benefits justify the cost is to ask whether the same benefits could have been accomplished at less cost. We are speaking here of redistribution of land ownership and redistribution of income from landowner to laborer. Let it be assumed that only income redistribution from former landowners to new landowners will be considered a benefit; that is, no redistribution from the rest of the economy will be considered a benefit. On this assumption we can calculate the savings to CORA. First, add the imputed wage of the *asentados* to the amount, estimated in Chapter 6, of redistribution they received from former landowners. Then subtract this sum from the actual receipts of the *asentamientos.* The total amount of cash income that would have accrued to the *asentados* of the seventeen sample asentamientos had they received the imputed wages and family allowances is $E°1,262,209.$[a] The amount actually received by them in advances plus profit shares was $E°2,677,606.$ The difference, when divided by the number of *asentados,* gives an average $E°2,538.$ Subtract the amount redistributed by former owners, $E°1,130,$ from the above average. The difference, $E°1,408,$ is the amount per *asentado* which is redistributed as income from the rest of the economy. If this amount is generalized to all 8,000 *asentados* of 1967, the redistribution of cash income to *asentados* from other sources in the economy is $E°13,264,000.$ A cut in *asentado* income by this amount would have decreased costs in 1967 by about 7.5 percent. Costs to the economy can, therefore, be cut by limiting *asentados'* income to the amount they would otherwise have received plus the amount redistributed from former owners. This can be achieved either by increasing the amount of redistribution or by decreasing the advances to *asentados.*

[a] This figure is slightly different from that of Chapter 6. It is adjusted for the family allowance share the government would have paid.

We can also examine how costs might be lowered through efforts to increase the amount of short-term capital repayments. There are several reasons for the nonrepayment of advances and production loans. One large item in production loans is paid labor from outside the farm. According to the law of agrarian reform, hiring labor except in an occasional way is illegal. The *asentamiento* is supposed to provide all its own permanent labor. If there is sufficient work to occupy more full-time laborers, then the number of *asentados* should be expanded. There is some evidence that the amount of labor hired is excessive. Such excess creates an unnecessary drain on resources. It is worth noting that there may be a conflict here between economic efficiency and social goals. There is every evidence that given present levels of development and supply of capital, the labor supply in Chile is overabundant. The agrarian reform may well serve to slow down the rate of exodus to the urban labor force until such time as that labor force can be absorbed by a faster-growing industrial sector.

A second major source of drain is that occasionally advances are made without consideration of the profitability of the farm, and in some cases without consideration of the number of days worked. There presumably needs to be some incentive to work. If advances are made on a regular monthly basis without regard to the number of days worked, and if no sanctions exist when the harvest does not yield enough to repay the advances, it is difficult to see where the incentive lies. There is one *asentamiento* in the sample where advances were given for all adult males in a family even though it was clear that the labor force needed for the farm was not even half the total number of families.

A third major drain on resources is also in the form of advances. CORA allowed some of the farms previously run on a sharecropping basis to remain that way. On these farms CORA makes advances for inputs and a maximum living allowance for particular crops. In other words, a maximum allowance is set for each hectare of wheat, another for each hectare of beans, etc. Three of the seventeen sample *asentamientos* were operated in this way. In all three of these cases the amount still owed CORA after the harvest was quite large.

CORA should find a way to operate by imposing proper sanctions such that at a minimum all production and subsistence advances are repaid with interest. If the farm is not run efficiently enough to make these repayments, it would be less costly simply to make transfer payments to *asentados*. A more serious effort should be made either to reduce the number of *asentados* to the number which will be supported on the farm, or to enlarge the number if the farm will support more.

Infrastructure constitutes another large cost. The *asentamiento* has so far avoided the costs of parcelization. If CORA assumes the cost of surveys, fences, and restructuring of irrigation facilities in those *asentamientos* which choose parcelization, costs will rise considerably. The major cost difference between the *asentamiento* organizational structure and the colonization projects of earlier laws lies in the infrastructure. This cost was nearly twice as much per family for these earlier colonies as it is for the *asentamientos*. Although CORA has made it clear that it wants to avoid these costs and has stressed the need for cooperation among *asentados* on the use of irrigation facilities and other infrastructure, it is not yet clear what the policy will be.

For an alternative cost calculation based on the above recommendations, we make the following assumptions. Sanctions are put in such a way that all production and subsistence allowances are repaid. Land payments after the initial down payment come from the *asentamiento* profits. Infrastructure costs are cut by 10 percent to allow for an estimated decrease in housing expenditure. Administrative costs are not changed. Under these assumptions costs for 1965–1970 could have been reduced about 40 percent.

It is not the purpose of this chapter to say to the Chileans what they should or should not do. Our purpose has been to put in perspective the costs associated with the reform and point out some method for reducing these costs.

**Summary and Conclusions**

It is often claimed that agrarian reform, by putting the control of land into the hands of those who work it, will provide the incentive to increased agricultural production. It is further claimed that such reform, by putting control over income in the hands of those who will spend it on domestic products, will thereby promote industrial growth through expanded markets. This sudy has investigated the ramifications of these hypotheses and has analyzed the degree to which the present agrarian reform in Chile is having and can have the results claimed.

In analyzing production we recognized two serious handicaps: (1) the time has been very short, and (2) the prereform data are at best only roughly accurate. However, we felt that the need for such a study was sufficiently strong to motivate whatever useful analysis was possible. Although recognizing the limitations of the data, we concluded that there was little, if any, change in production by 1967 on farms affected by the reform.

This statement is in opposition to claims usually made by CORA. There is no doubt that production on some *asentamientos* has increased, but it has declined or remained the same on others. CORA naturally tends to concentrate attention on those *asentamientos* whose output has increased. This study used more objective data than is used by CORA in evaluating production changes. It is, of course, recognized that the sample was small and that the variability among *asentamientos* is large. We therefore do not state positively that there has been no change, but rather that there is insufficient evidence to support a claim that there has been a change.[1]

The amount of income that will be distributed by the reform is dependent on two factors: the rate of inflation and the profit rate on the farm prior to expropriation. Since only a part of the indemnification is adjusted for the cost of living, the higher the inflation rate the greater the amount of redistribution. The difference between the real interest rate paid and the profit rate which would have been earned had the farm not been expropriated measures the redistribution effect. Unless farms expropriated after 1967 have a higher prereform rate of profit than those expropriated prior to 1967, the amount of redistribution is probably not sufficient to be felt in the industrial sector. However, the analysis provided reason to expect that expropriation of farms after 1967 will in fact result in a greater amount of redistributed income. In this case it is reasonable to expect that the effect on demand will be felt in the industrial sector. Even so, the effect will be small. Further, knowledge of production functions and of the current level of operation for particular industries would be required to predict the effect of this demand shift on incentive to innovate.

It is appropriate to ask whether or not this study has any significance for agrarian reform policy in other Latin American countries. This question can be answered in the affirmative. Several important issues that relate to all agrarian reforms were examined here. First, the current structure of tenancy must be examined before it is assumed that production will be increased by a reform. Unless the mode of tenancy is predominantly that of sharecropping, it is not so clear that the motivation for increasing production will be present. In particular, if the cultural pattern gives status to a landowner with resident laborers, land redistribution may simply perpetuate this system on a smaller scale. A structure such as the *asentamiento could* be used as a method to influence such cultural behavior. But such a structure requires that the administrative personnel take deliberate measures to effect such changes.

A second issue with relevance to other countries is that of income redistribution. In the Chilean case, at least on present reform farms, there is a greater amount of redistribution to new landowners from other sectors of the economy than from previous landowners. It is one thing for the government to transfer funds from another sector of the economy for agricultural investment. It is quite another to transfer funds as income. The question must be raised whether or not such a transfer is an improvement. The demands for agrarian reform as social change have been couched in terms of the redistribution from landlords to workers and not from the urban to the rural sector. In formulating policy for agrarian reform, politicians should face squarely the issue of the source of the redistribution.

Finally, it is relevant to policy makers of agrarian reforms in other countries to have brought to their attention the importance of analyzing the budget patterns of those from whom and to whom income is redistributed. A reform which is significant enough to have an impact on demand in the industrial sector may also affect savings. Even if savings do not decline, there will be a need to develop a mechanism for transfering these savings to the industrial sector.

## Appendix A:

## Absolute and Relative Wheat Prices, 1942–1964

| Year | Wheat Prices in Current $E^0$ | Wheat Prices/ Cost of Living | Wheat Prices/ Nonlivestock Agricultural Prices |
|------|------|------|------|
| 1942 | 154 | 1.27 | 1.08 |
| 1943 | 165 | 1.18 | 1.07 |
| 1944 | 169 | 1.05 | 1.05 |
| 1945 | 178 | 1.05 | 0.98 |
| 1946 | 217 | 1.09 | 1.00 |
| 1947 | 300 | 1.13 | 1.01 |
| 1948 | 373 | 1.18 | 1.08 |
| 1949 | 403 | 1.07 | 1.11 |
| 1950 | 416 | 0.97 | 0.97 |
| 1951 | 512 | 0.97 | 0.88 |
| 1952 | 711 | 1.10 | 0.87 |
| 1953 | 860 | 1.06 | 0.90 |
| 1954 | 1,254 | 0.90 | 0.89 |
| 1955 | 1,967 | 0.81 | 0.88 |
| 1956 | 2,841 | 0.75 | 0.80 |
| 1957 | 4,510 | 0.89 | 0.83 |
| 1958 | 6,054 | 1.00 | 1.09 |
| 1959 | 7,058 | 0.84 | 0.91 |
| 1960 | 7,703 | 0.83 | 0.80 |
| 1961 | 7,778 | 0.77 | 0.84 |
| 1962 | 9,011 | 0.79 | 0.86 |
| 1963 | 12,230 | 0.74 | 0.84 |
| 1964 | 18,033 | 0.75 | 0.84 |

Source: Direccion de Estadistice y Censos, *Estadistics Chilena*, Santiago, 1940–1964.

## Appendix B:

## Acreage and Prices for All Agriculture, 1940–1959

| Year | Index of Total Acreage [a] | Index of Agricultural Price Deflated by Cost of Living [b] | Output/Input Prices [c] (1951 = 100) |
|------|------|------|------|
| 1940 | 97.0 | 100.0 | |
| 1941 | 90.7 | 103.7 | |
| 1942 | 94.6 | 99.9 | |
| 1943 | 98.3 | 94.8 | |
| 1944 | 100.3 | 102.2 | |
| 1945 | 90.6 | 125.0 | |
| 1946 | 93.1 | 118.8 | 75.9 |
| 1947 | 94.6 | 129.1 | 82.2 |
| 1948 | 98.2 | 117.2 | 81.1 |
| 1949 | 97.0 | 116.2 | 85.3 |
| 1950 | 100.0 | 120.2 | 92.9 |
| 1951 | 99.2 | 123.0 | 96.6 |
| 1952 | 97.5 | 137.4 | 98.4 |
| 1953 | 98.2 | 130.0 | 85.8 |
| 1954 | 99.9 | 117.4 | 105.2 |
| 1955 | 98.8 | 106.0 | 110.2 |
| 1956 | 106.1 | 100.2 | 103.7 |
| 1957 | 107.1 | 106.3 | 95.7 |
| 1958 | 104.0 | 91.3 | 95.5 |
| 1959 | 110.6 | 90.2 | 93.0 |

Sources:

[a] *La Economica de Chile en El Periodo 1950–1963*, p. 69, and *Estadistica Chilena*, 1940–1964.

[b] *La Economia de Chile en El Periodo 1950–1963*, p. 72.

[c] Markos Mamalakis and Clark Reynolds, *Essays on the Chilean Economy* (Homewood: Richard D. Irwin, 1965), p. 136; and Kurt Ulrich and Ricardo Lagos, *Agricultura y Tributacion* (Santiago: Universidad de Chile, 1965), p. 32.

**Appendix C:**

**Wheat Acreage in Five Provinces and All Chile, 1942–1943 to 1963–1964 (in 1000 Hectares)**

| Year | Coquimbo | Santiago | O'Higgins | Colchagua | Cautin | Chile |
|------|----------|----------|-----------|-----------|--------|-------|
| 1942 | 20.0 | 42.0 | 21.0 | 30.0 | 134.4 | 750.6 |
| 1943 | 19.6 | 46.8 | 21.7 | 28.2 | 146.9 | 797.3 |
| 1944 | 22.8 | 42.6 | 18.1 | 26.3 | 143.5 | 801.4 |
| 1945 | 12.1 | 41.4 | 17.2 | 27.5 | 141.1 | 727.8 |
| 1946 | 15.0 | 24.6 | 17.3 | 28.5 | 146.5 | 757.9 |
| 1947 | 17.4 | 38.8 | 19.2 | 37.7 | 151.1 | 818.7 |
| 1948 | 22.1 | 46.3 | 17.7 | 35.4 | 151.6 | 867.4 |
| 1949 | 25.0 | 60.4 | 19.0 | 35.9 | 152.7 | 833.2 |
| 1950 | 25.0 | 49.6 | 22.5 | 39.2 | 153.8 | 816.0 |
| 1951 | 19.8 | 57.6 | 28.8 | 36.4 | 131.9 | 762.3 |
| 1952 | 21.4 | 47.8 | 23.6 | 37.5 | 143.7 | 779.1 |
| 1953 | 21.1 | 51.2 | 19.2 | 35.0 | 136.3 | 761.4 |
| 1954 | 24.4 | 42.4 | 20.5 | 30.8 | 138.8 | 762.2 |
| 1955 | 22.6 | 43.0 | 18.5 | 34.7 | 142.6 | 776.8 |
| 1956 | 21.8 | 44.2 | 17.8 | 35.0 | 114.9 | 766.5 |
| 1957 | 23.0 | 46.7 | 18.8 | 37.0 | 121.3 | 807.2 |
| 1958 | 27.5 | 52.2 | 26.7 | 46.5 | 165.1 | 893.8 |
| 1959 | 28.8 | 56.8 | 22.3 | 44.6 | 166.2 | 889.0 |
| 1960 | 19.9 | 54.1 | 22.9 | 46.2 | 159.5 | 838.0 |
| 1961 | 25.8 | 59.7 | 22.0 | 47.1 | 152.9 | 849.3 |
| 1962 | 25.6 | 59.9 | 22.2 | 45.5 | 149.9 | 843.2 |
| 1963 | 27.9 | 57.0 | 22.6 | 45.3 | 147.8 | |

Source: *Estadistica Chilena*, 1940–1964.

# Bibliography

# Bibliography

## Public Documents

Banco Central de Chile. *Boletin Mensual.* Santiago, 1950–1968.

Committee of Nine for the Alliance for Progress. *Evaluacion del Programa Nacional de Desarrollo Economica y Social de Chile.* Report of the ad hoc committee presented to the government of Chile. Santiago, 1962.

CORA. *El Asentamiento.* Santiago, 1967.

Direccion de Estadistica y Censos. Republica de Chile. *Estadistica Chilena.* Santiago, 1940–1964.

Direccion de Estadistica y Censos. *Industrias Manufactureros.* Santiago, 1960–1966.

Direccion de Estadistica y Censos. *IV Censo Nacional Agropecuaria.* Santiago, 1966.

Direccion General de la Produccion Agraria y Pesquera. *La Agricultura Chilena en el Quinquenio, 1951–1955.* Santiago, 1957.

Food and Agricultural Organization of the United Nations and Instituto de Capacitacion e Investigacion en Reforma Agraria. *Evaluacion Preliminar de Los Asentamientos de La Reforma Agraria de Chile.* Santiago, 1967.

Food and Agricultural Organization of the United Nations and Instituto de Capacitacion e Investigacion en Reforma Agraria. *Fertilizers, An Annual Review of World Production, Consumption, and Trade.* Rome, 1966.

International Bank for Reconstruction and Development. *The Agricultural Economy of Chile.* Washington, 1962.

*La Verdad Sobre La Reforma Agraria.* Santiago: Editorial del Pacifico, S.A., 1967.

Oficina de Planificacion Nacional. *Indice de Produccion Agropecuaria-Silvicola, 1939–1964.* Santiago, 1966.

Oficina de Plainificacion Nacional. "Cuentas Nacionales, 1960–1966." Mimeographed. Santiago, 1967.

Republica de Chile. Ley No. 16,640. *Reforma Agraria.* 1967.

United Nations, Department of Economic Affairs. *Land Reform: Defects in Agrarian Structure as Obstacles to Economic Development.* New York, 1951.

United Nations, Economic and Social Council. *Progress in Land Reform: Fourth Report* (E/4020). New York, 1965.

U.S. Department of Agriculture, Farm Economic Division. *Agrarian Reform and Economic Growth.* Washington, 1962.


## Books

Aldunate, Paul. *Sistemas de Participacion en Las Empresas Agricolas: Caracteristicas Economicas y Determinacion de Tipos.* Santiago: Catholic University of Chile, 1968.

Aldunate, Paul. *A Study of the Use of Resources and the Economic Result of Agricultural Firms from the Central Valley of Chile*. Santiago: Catholic University of Chile, 1967.

Barbero, G. *Land Reform in Italy*. Rome: FAO, 1961.

Bennett, Peter D. *Government's Role in Retail Marketing of Food Products in Chile*. Austin: University of Texas, 1968.

Bray, James. *La Intensidad del Uso de la Tierra en Relacion con el Tamaño de los Predios en el Valle Central de Chile*. Santiago: Center for Economic Research, Universidad de Chile, 1960.

Comite Interamericano de Desarrollo Agricola. *Tenencia de la Tierra y Desarrollo Socio-económico del Sector Agrícola*. Santiago: ICIRA, 1966.

Delgado, Oscar, ed. *Reformas Agrarias en La America Latina*. Mexico: Fondo De Cultura Economica, 1965.

Ellsworth, P. T. *Chile, An Economy in Transition*. New York: The Macmillan Co., 1945.

Johnston, J. *Econometric Methods*. New York: McGraw Hill, 1963.

Mamalakis, Markos, and Reynolds, Clark. *Essays on the Chilean Economy*. Homewood: Richard D. Irwin, Inc., 1965.

Martellaro, Joseph. *Economic Development in Southern Italy*. Washington: The Catholic U. of America Press, 1965.

Munoz, Oscar. *Crecimiento Industrial de Chile, 1914–1965*. Santiago: Universidad de Chile, 1968.

Nerlove, Marc. *The Dynamics of Supply: Estimation of Farmers' Response to Price*. Baltimore: Johns Hopkins, 1958.

Ramirez, Pablo. *Cambio en Las Formas de Pago a la Mano de Obra Agricola*. Santiago: ICIRA, 1968.

Scheytman, Alexander. *El Inquilino del Valle Central*. Santiago: ICIRA, 1968.

Schultz, Theodore. *Transforming Traditional Agriculture*. New Haven: Yale University Press, 1964.

Thiesenhusen, William. *Chile's Experiments in Agrarian Reform*. Madison: University of Wisconsin Press, 1966.

Tuma, Elias. *Twenty-six Centuries of Agrarian Reform*. Berkeley: U. of California Press, 1965.

Ulrich, Kurt, and Lagos, Ricardo. *La Agricultura y Tributacion*. Santiago: Universidad de Chile, 1965.

Universidad de Chile, Instituto de Economia. *Demanda de Bienes Durables: Gran Santiago*. Santiago, 1965.

Universidad de Chile, Instituto de Economia. *La Economia de Chile en el Periodo 1950–1963*. 2 vols. Santiago, 1963.

Universidad de Chile, Instituto de Economia. *Ocupacion y Desocupacion Gran Santiago*. Santiago, 1956–1968.

Universidad de Chile, Instituto de Economia. *Utilizacion de la Capacidad Instalada en 42 Empresos Industriales*. Santiago, 1963.

Valdes, Alberto. *Costos, Ingresos y Diferenciales de Salararios en Dos Provincias Agricolas.* Santiago: Catholic University of Chile, 1967.

Warriner, Doreen. *Land Reform and Economic Development in the Middle East.* New York: Oxford University Press, 1962.


**Articles and Periodicals**

Becket, James. "Land Reform in Chile." *Journal of Interamerican Studies* 5 (April 1963): 177–188.

Chonchol, Jacques. "La Reforma Agraria en America Latina." In proceedings of the Escuela de Invierno de La Universidad de Chile 1 (July 1963): 71–75.

Dorner, Peter. "Land Tenure, Income Distribution, and Productivity Interactions." *Land Economics* 40, No. 3 (August 1964): 247–254.

Felix, David. "Agrarian Reform and Industrial Growth." *International Development Review* 1, No. 2 (October 1960): 16–22.


**Unpublished Material**

Aldunate, Paul. "A Comparison of Resource Productivities and Efficiency on Private and Government-Created Farms in the Central Valley of Chile." M.S. thesis, Department of Agricultural Economics, Purdue University, 1965.

Arak, Marcelle. "The Supply of Brazilian Coffee." Ph.D. thesis, Department of Economics, MIT, 1967.

Barraclough, Solon. "Agricultural Policy and Land Reform." Unpublished paper given at the Conference on Key Problems of Economic Policy in Latin America, University of Chicago, November 1966.

Behrman, Jere R. "Supply Response in Underdeveloped Agriculture: A Case Study of Four Major Annual Crops in Thailand." Ph.D. thesis, Department of Economics, MIT, 1966.

Collarte, Juan. "Analisis de una Alternativa de los Sistemas de Tenencia en Chile." Thesis for the title of *Engeniero Agronomo,* University of Chile, 1964.

Fonck, Carlos. "An Estimate of Agricultural Resource Productivities by Using Aggregate Production Functions, Chile, 1954–1955." M.S. thesis, Department of Agricultural Economics, Cornell University, 1966.

Garcia, Eduardo. "Inflation in Chile, a Quantitative Analysis." Ph.D. thesis, Department of Economics, MIT, 1964.

Imable, Rogelio. "Cambios en Los Ingresos de Campesinos Chilenos Participantes en Reforma Agraria." Unpublished Memoria de Prueba, Department of Economics, University of Chile, 1967.

118

INPROA. "Evaluacion del Proceso de Reforma Agraria del Instituto de Promocion Agraria." Santiago, 1966.

Morales, Hector. "Productividad Presente y Potencial en 96 Predios de la Provincia de O'Higgins y su Relacion con el Tamaño de los Propiedades." Thesis for the title of *Engeniero Agronomo,* University of Chile, 1964.

Rosenstein-Rodan, Paul. "Remarks on the Economic Effects of Agrarian Reform." Unpublished paper prepared by the Center for International Studies, MIT, 1954.

Sternberg, Marvin J. "Chilean Land Tenure and Land Reform." Ph.D. thesis, Department of Economics, University of California at Berkeley, 1962.

# Notes

# Notes

## Chapter 1
## Introduction

1. Jacques Chonchol, "La Reforma Agraria en America Latina," in *Escuela de Invierno de la Universidad de Chile*. All translations of Spanish texts in this paper are mine.

2. See, for example: U.N. Department of Economic Affairs, *Land Reform: Defects in Agrarian Structure as Obstacles to Economic Development* (New York, 1951); and Solon Barraclough, "Agricultural Policy and Land Reform," unpublished paper given at the Conference on Key Problems of Economic Policy in Latin America; University of Chicago, November, 1966.

3. Jere Behrman, in "Supply Response in Underdeveloped Agriculture: A Case Study of Four Major Annual Crops in Thailand, 1937–1963" (Ph.D. thesis, Department of Economics, MIT, 1966), p. 20, gives a summary of previous studies made of supply responsiveness. His own study makes a further contribution in this area.

4. See Theodore Schultz, *Transforming Traditional Agriculture* (New Haven: Yale University Press, 1964), pp. 119–120, for arguments on the rationality of farmers. Schultz does argue, however, that absentee arrangements are inefficient.

5. Marcelle Arak, "The Supply of Brazilian Coffee" (Ph.D. thesis, Department of Economics, MIT, 1967). This study could find no sensitivity in the response of new land to price changes: see p. 135.

6. Behrman, op. cit., pp. 84–93.

7. Paul Rosenstein-Rodan, "Remarks on Economic Effects of Agrarian Reform," CENIS, MIT, 1954.

8. In the study of Marvin Sternberg, "Chilean Land Tenure and Land Reform" (Ph.D. thesis, University of California, Berkeley, 1962), he estimates the average net income of the twenty landowners interviewed at about $50,000 in 1960. Paul Aldunate, in *A Study of the Use of Resources and the Economic Result of Agricultural Firms from the Central Valley of Chile* (Santiago: Catholic University of Chile, 1967), estimates the average income in 1967 at E°160,000, or something over $30,000.

9. Barraclough, op. cit., p. 44.

10. Doreen Warriner, in *Land Reform and Economic Development in the Middle East* (New York: Oxford University Press, 1962), argues that the Egyptian reform was primarily a measure to redistribute political power. In Mexico and Bolivia the reforms appeared to be merely pacification schemes to preserve the social order.

## Chapter 2
## The Agricultural Sector of Chile

1. National Planning Office (ODEPLAN), *Indice De Produccion Agropecuaria-Silvicola, 1939–1964,* Santiago, 1966.

2. The estimates for the percent of land and value of production in this section are taken from Comite Interamericano de Desarrollo Agricola, *Chile: Tenencia de la Tierra y Desarrollo Socio-Economico del Sector Agricola,* Santiago: ICIRA, 1966. This work will henceforth be referred to as the CIDA Report. It is a report of a committee formed by various U.S. organizations, the Organization of American States, and the Interamerican Development Bank.

3. Universidad de Chile, Instituto de Economia, *La Economia de Chile en el Periodo 1950–1963,* II (Santiago, 1963), p. 15.

4. Ibid., for the figures from 1940 and 1960. Those for 1965 are from the revision of GNP estimates by ODEPLAN.

5. See Universidad de Chile: Instituto de Economia y Planificacion, *Ocupacion y Desocupacion,* Santiago, published since 1956 for estimates on unemployment.

6. *La Economia de Chile en el Perioda 1950–1963,* I, 97.

7. See Peter Bennett, *Government's Role in Retail Marketing of Food Products in Chile* (Austin: University of Texas, 1968) for a description of the detailed checks on price and quality made at every level in the sale of wheat and wheat products.

8. *La Economia de Chile en el Periodo 1950–1963,* p. 97; see also Ricardo Lagos, "Tributacion," in *La Agricultura y Tributacion,* ed. Kurt Ulrich and Ricardo Lagos (Santiago: Universidad de Chile, 1965), p. 68.

9. Lagos, op. cit., p. 69.

10. *La Economia de Chile en el Periodo, 1950–1963,* I, 98.

11. Markos Mamalakis and Clark Reynolds, *Essays on the Chilean Economy* (Homewood: Richard D. Irwin, 1965), p. 145.

12. Oscar Delgado, in *Reformas Agrarias en America Latina* (Mexico: Fondo De Cultura Economica, 1965) gives various arguments on either side of this discussion.

13. *La Verdad Sobre La Reforma Agraria* (Santiago: Editorial del Pacifico, S.A., 1967), p. 1 This booklet is distributed by CORA.

14. See the following studies on this issue: James O. Bray, *La Intensidad del Uso de la Tierra en Relacion con el Tamaño de los Predios en el Valle Central de Chile,* (Santiago: Center for Economic Research, Universidad de Chile, 1960); Hector Morales, "Productividad Presente y Potencial en 96 Predios en la Provincia de O'Higgins y su Relacion con el Tamaño de los Propriedades" (thesis presented for the degree of Agricultural Engineer, University of Chile, 1964); and David Baytelman and

Rolando Chateauneuf, "Interpretacion del Censo Agricola y Ganadero de 1955," in *Panorama Economica,* 14 (September, 1960), pp. 165–166.

15. Instituto de Investigacion de Recursos Naturales, *Potencialidad Agricola de Las Provincias de Tarapaca a Llanquihue Segun Estratificacion de Predios Por Avaluo y Superficie,* Santiago, 1967.

16. CIDA, p. 180.

17. Mamalakis, op. cit., pp. 117–148.

18. Ibid., p. 143.

19. Marc Nerlove, *The Dynamics of Supply: Estimation of Farmers' Response to Price* (Baltimore: Johns Hopkins Press, 1958).

20. Behrman, op. cit.

21. See J. Johnston, *Econometric Methods* (New York: McGraw-Hill, 1963), pp. 211–221.

22. G. Hildreth and J. J. Lu, "Demand Relations with Auto-Correlated Disturbances," Michigan State University Agricultural Experiment Station, Technical Bulletin No. 276, 1960.

23. Phillip Cooper, "Notes on Procedures for Linear Regression in the Presence of First Order Serially Correlated Disturbances" (unpublished report, MIT, 1968).

24. IBRD, *The Agricultural Economy of Chile* (Washington, 1952), p. 122; and CIDA, pp. 173–178.

**Chapter 3**
**History of the Legal Institutions for**
**Agrarian Reform**

1. The data on previous laws and their application in this chapter are taken from the CIDA report, pp. 248–252.

2. William Thiesenhusen, in *Chile's Experiments in Agrarian Reform* (Madison: University of Wisconsin Press, 1966), has described, analyzed, and criticized this program of INPROA.

3. See Ricardo Lagos, "Tributacion," in *La Agricultura y Tributacion,* ed. Kurt Ulrich and Ricardo Lagos (Santiago: Universidad de Chile, 1965) for an evaluation of the difference between the fiscal and the commercial values of farms up to 1962. In that year an index based on 1940 = 100 showed the fiscal value in the area of 5000 and the commercial value to be about 13000. However, with the project air-photograph, a new evaluation was made in 1965 which Lagos, in the appendix to his essay, indicates is much closer to the commercial value, but he does not estimate how close. Observers claimed in 1966 that the fiscal value was equal to about 80% of the commercial value.

## Chapter 4
## Case Study of an Individual Asentamiento

1. Alberto Valdés, "Costos, Ingresos y Diferencialés de Salarios in Dos Provincias Agricolas" (Center for Economic Research: Catholic University of Chile, 1967), p. 8.

2. Pablo Ramirez, *Cambio en Las Formas de Pago a le Mano de Obra Agricola,* Santiago: ICIRA, 1968, p. 29.

## Chapter 5
## Production on Asentamientos

1. Banco Central de Chile, "Boletin Mensual," #486, August, 1968, p. 711, gives the figures on plantings and harvest. Calculations on productivity are made by the author.

2. Unpublished report by INPROA, "Evaluacion del Proceso de Reforma Agraria del Instituto de Promocion Agraria," Santiago, Chile, 1965, p. 10.

3. William Thiesenhusen, in *Chile's Experiments in Agrarian Reform* (Madison: University of Wisconsin Press, 1966), pp. 120, 158, states that these data are unavailable.

4. See the CIDA report, p. 147, and Chapter 2 of this work. The relevant comparison is with family-size, not with less than family-size farms.

5. Paul Aldunate, "A Comparison of Resource Productivity and Efficiency on Private and Government-Created Farms in the Central Valley of Chile" (Master's thesis, Department of Agricultural Economics, Purdue University, 1965).

## Chapter 6
## Impact of Income Redistribution:
## Savings and Demand Shifts

1. Marvin J. Sternberg, "Chilean Land Tenure and Land Reform" (Ph.D. thesis, Department of Economics, University of California at Berkely, 1962).

2. Pablo Ramirez, *Cambio en Las Formas de Pago a la Mano de Obra Agricola* (Santiago: ICIRA, 1968).

3. For example, Alberto Valdes, in *Costos, Ingresos y Diferenciales de Salarios en Dos Provincias Agricolas* (Santiago: 1967), estimated the opportunity cost of land paid in kind to *inquilinos* as E°1.92. Adjusting

this to E° of 1967, and allowing a value of E°1.5 for the value of the garden plot we arrive at the figures used.

4. Ramirez, op. cit., p. 35.
5. Sternberg, op. cit., p. 89.
6. Ibid.
7. Markos Mamalakis and Clark Reynolds, *Essays on the Chilean Economy* (Homewood: Richard D. Irwin, 1965), pp. 149–168.
8. Direccion de Estadistica y Censos, *Industrias Manufactureros,* Santiago, 1966.
9. The CIDA report, pp. 161, 187.

## Chapter 7
### Ideal Versus Reality

1. See objective #2 of the *asentamiento* as established in the law: to train members in the responsibility of being farm managers.

## Chapter 8
### Costs and Alternatives

1. See, for example, the paper presented by Clark Reynolds, "Ideology and Economic Development in Mexico," to the American Association for the Advancement of Science Symposium on Ideology and Social Change in Latin America, Dallas, Texas, December 30, 1968.

## Chapter 9
### Summary and Conclusions

1. Richard Meyer, in a Ph.D. dissertation completed in February, 1970 on "Debt Repayment Capacity of the Chilean Agrarian Reform Benefici-aries" (Cornell University: Latin American Studies Program Dissertation Series Number 14) carefully selected six *asentamientos* for intensive study. On five of these six, net farm income increased from 1966/67 to 1967/68. These results lend credence to the possibility that after more experience with *asentamiento* operation, more output can be expected.